How I F***ed Up My Life and Made It Mean Something

BENJAMIN FRY

Khiron Books

Printed in the United Kingdom

Khiron Books
10 Harley Street,
London W1G 9PF

+44 (0)20 7467 8368

www.khironbooks.com

First Edition, April 2014

ISBN: 1494473747
ISBN-13: 978-1494473747

14 13 12 11 10 / 10 9 8 7 6 5 4 3 2 1

DEDICATION

To my many healers who saved me

To Inca, Theo, Melina, Aurelia and David
who gave them that chance

To Stavroula-Dorothea Maraki
who gave them to me

CONTENTS

ACKNOWLEDGMENTS

I would like to thank my editor, friend and book writing mentor Candida Crewe who shepherded this book into production from a very rough manuscript; Maureen Rice for her peerless vision of how to place content in a modern world; those who helped me along the way generally in my life, through my recovery and during the work which has brought me this far and which continues; as well as my family for putting up with me all along.

1 INTRODUCTION

I didn't want to write this book. Having written it, I didn't want to read it. Having read it, I didn't want to publish it. It won't take you long to figure out why.

If you have ever suffered from something described as 'mental illness' or 'a personality disorder' or an 'addiction' then you will want to read this book.

If you have ever been to a therapist, or a psychologist, or a doctor, or a psychiatrist, desperate for help, willing to do whatever it takes, wanting to believe that they know what they are doing, but coming to realise that, deep down, they are just as lost as you, then you will want to read this book.

If you have ever submitted yourself to treatment, in a hospital, or a rehab, or just to a practitioner healing you with words or medication, and wanted more than anything for it to work, but found them worse than the original problem, then you will want to read this book.

If you have had friends and family, who loved you and wanted to help you, but had no idea how to and sometimes ended up making things worse, then you will want to read this book.

If everyone around you had an opinion, all of them different, none of them right but all of them wishing that you thought that they were, then you will want to read this book.

If you were ever lost, desperately utterly lost, but more than anything just wanted to find your way home, more than anything wanted someone, anyone to tell you what was wrong with you and how to get better, then you absolutely, definitely, must read this book.

There is an epidemic in our modern society of so-called addictions, disorders and poor mental health. This is talked about as a problem with our minds, something you can't see or touch, something therefore very hard to 'treat'.

But the truth is much more simple.

A new paradigm of understanding of all of these conditions is emerging and, from that new understanding, new treatments are emerging, which aim to cure, not just to treat.

Pseudo-science is giving way to real science. Placebo treatments are being replaced by accurate methods leading to effective results. Despair is giving way to hope.

This is the first of three books. The second will explain this new understanding in detail and give you a self-help guide to implementing it at home. The third will describe how these problems have hijacked our world, our families, relationships, communities, culture and planet.

But first I have to tell you my story. For how else would you know that I'm telling you the truth?

1 BACKSTORY

I seemed like an unlikely person to end up forty years old, impossibly in debt, desperately trying not to take my own life in a mental hospital, alone, thousands of miles from home. I was talented, educated, well-resourced and connected. I had had a perfect start in life. On paper.

Beneath this invulnerable supremacy of my external self, emerging into adult life, was the wasteland of my early psychological self. This was not part of my story; my family did not discuss it, I did not discuss it, and in fact I barely could even think about it. I had grown up in a climate of denial and fear, ruled by taboo and the cold panic around unpalatable reactions in the family dynamic.

I was not in fact the child of my mother and father, nor true sibling of my younger twin brother and sister. My nuclear English family was a lie. There was a whole story which came before the union of the parents I grew up with; a short but fairly savagely dramatic one. My parents met, I'm told, at a wedding, where my father in typically charismatic style went up to my mother, a twenty year-old American visiting friends, and asked her to remove her hat so that he could more clearly see her eyes. This is the kind of story a child likes to hear from his parents, but I got it second hand. My father and I have only spoken once or twice about my mother and with great discomfort some time in my twenties. It always felt very taboo, or perhaps was just too difficult for him, or even maybe just for me.

She came from a Camelot type family herself in New England. Her mother was an identical twin and these two women married into rich, well-established local families, almost in a race with each other to enact the perfect American fairy tale of the times. Between the two sisters they had seven children, my mother the youngest but one by three weeks. The families appeared to have all the charms that life could bring. They had intellect, looks, sporting prowess, money, connections and position. My father married into this and was quite taken with this glamorous whirl of foreign life. Inevitably, there were cracks beneath the surface. My mother's father was allegedly too fond of the drink, from a line of rumoured alcoholics; tensions in the family were carefully muted; and the story went that my mother was the peacemaker, that she was the one who held it all together.

A few months after my birth in Guildford, in England, her first child at twenty-four, she was given a terminal diagnosis of aplastic anaemia, a bone marrow problem much like leukaemia which even now is often fatal. This vibrant, beautiful young woman, from a fine American dynasty, with a charming, charismatic entrepreneurial and sporting husband was dying; just weeks, really, after giving birth to me. As I now know well from my own story, reversals in life for the privileged are hard in their own way, and the impression I have is that she and her family didn't really deal with it at all. Instead they seemed to do what rich people often do, which is to continue with plan A and to throw money at the problem. My mother was whisked back to America from London , to her parents' beach-side house in Newport, Rhode Island, and from there made visits to a doctor in Boston who claimed to have a cure for this – (as it was then) incurable disease. Shortly after my eighteenth birthday, my mother's best-friend took me out to lunch. She gave me my mother's wedding ring, which had been entrusted to her by, I think, my father. I asked her why there was nothing else left to me, why there was no note? Her answer took me by surprise: my mother never really thought that she was dying.

I can relate to this. In what follows you will see that reality, for some from such a gifted and cosseted background, is a very, very hard bite to swallow, not least when it doesn't fit the fairy tale paradigm. Then, it is particularly haunting, feared and repelled. It is not impossible to imagine how a group of young people in their twenties, along with their sozzelled and stressed relations could bury deep in their psyches the unpalatable reality that one of the cherished, younger members of their family was going to die.

So there seemed to be little preparation for the inevitable. This was something which I would come back to time and time again, in ever increasingly ghastly ways, during the course of my own recovery.

The band simply played on, and then one day, on her twenty-fifth birthday, my mother lapsed into a coma. My father had to fly back from England to turn off her life support system, and then she was gone.

I was left in Newport that summer, possibly for four to five weeks. I was eleven months old. No-one seems to be able to remember who was in charge of me. The best guess is a dynastically available nanny. My father returned to England and moved in with a woman he met on the flight home. I eventually returned to England with my inconsolable grandmother and was left at the Hampshire home of another of my mother's friends, who also had an adopted little girl slightly older than me. I suppose the idea was to simulate some form of family life, and perhaps it worked. However the reports of my condition at the time (it was shortly after my first birthday) are shocking. I was unable to eat and refused food. They were worried that I would have to be hospitalised. The father of the family was able to force feed me, apparently, sparing me more severe treatment. My adopted sister from that time has in adult life described her memories and family stories of this time quite vividly.

"I do remember how traumatised you were when you first came to us, and with good reason, you had just lost your mother. You refused to eat for a very long time, and you were terribly, terribly withdrawn, but you did slowly come out of your shell and later memories are all of playing and me teaching you how to climb out of your cot and be naughty with me (I always got the blame though!) I used to roll a wastepaper bin up to the side, climb up and haul you over the top!"

That shell and this time in general would come back to haunt me. Over the next year my father rebuilt his life, visiting me apparently at weekends, and got into a relationship with a new woman, his soon-to-be second wife, which has lasted over forty years. After a while I went to live with them in London, in Ladbroke Grove; I think I was nearly two. This could have been an ideal stabilising feature in my life: a long happy marriage and a new family. My new 'mother' had her own children by my father when I was nearly six, a twin boy and girl, and then we were a perfect family. And that is how it remained. No one ever mentioned my mother, or the traumatic history for either my father or myself of those first two years of my life.

It is perhaps not completely mystifying that this happened. This was a time (the early 1970s) when feelings were not the currency of everyday magazine articles and my father and new mother were the children of a stoical post-war generation. Amateur psychologists of the time would have been readily able to argue that the best thing was not to talk about it. However, in later life, when I did bring up the subject, with a great deal of trepidation and difficulty, it was clear that it was very, very hard to integrate the reality of my first family into a new family dynamic which appeared to have clung onto denial in order to survive. The ghost of the perfect dead wife did not appear to sit easily with the second wife, and her own difficulties were such that anything which didn't sit easily with her was in turn threatening for my father, my siblings and myself. No, I was on my own with this one, and so it remained.

My father was public school and Oxford educated

and fantastically capable at operating in the world as a 'businessman'. People ask what that means exactly, but most people have an idea. He makes money by making money and that's as good a trade as any, I suppose. I grew up somewhat sheltered from the ups and downs of his elastic entrepreneurism. I remember only one period of childhood when money seemed to be a difficult issue, and really only one occasion when a small request seemed to cause some resistance. Generally my impression was of being provided for – a comfortable home, food, toys and clothes on demand, and private schools including a boarding school from the age of eight, and Eton.

I had no perspective on this because this was the same as everyone else I knew from my private schools. Money seemed to be the birth-right of those who were in this club. We didn't really have poor friends or relations. Our lives were a fairly homogeneous spread of very similar people. My father's great other love after money was cricket. Again this world seemed to come with a fairly gilded heritage. No-one seemed to struggle. Good things and the good life just seemed to be factory-fitted.

On top of all of this I was genuinely gifted myself in various, crucial aspects of schoolboy currency. I appeared to be rich in a way which money could not buy. I was ok at sport, good at music, socially successful, certainly good looking (in my youth!) and above all much, much cleverer than I seemed to let on to my teachers. In later years I would come to understand that my early years had blunted my cognition and memory, but beneath that was a furiously able analytical mind. This was a heady combination. Among the most privileged elite of the most privileged society on earth, I was one of the more naturally gifted of that circle. An easy life seemed to beckon. What could possibly go wrong? It never occurred to me ever to ask that question.

My father's career really blossomed along with my adolescence. He was himself a mixture of fortunes by background. His parents scrimped and saved to send him and his two brothers to a boarding school and they all went to Oxford, but they started their adult lives penniless and in that sense he is a proudly self-made man. His father was a BBC journalist and for a while ran a hotel on the Beaulieu River in Hampshire.]. They were neither posh nor downtrodden, but solidly 'middle class'. My father became extremely rich by these standards in my late teens and so in many ways my gilded package was complete. We had lavish holidays, two large comfortable houses, one in central London and another for weekends in Wiltshire and none of the ordinary things that any family might want to do such as going out for a meal, classes for the kids, clothing, presents and parties were in any way too expensive.

This might seem like a full cup with which to leave school. Indeed, I actually left Eton in my own brand new car, a red convertible Golf. I had in my back pocket a place at Oxford University to take up in 15 months' time and it seemed as if my life could only ever be charmed. Even by my standards this flush of fortune did not pass me by. I felt blessed, gifted and lucky. Even by the standards of my fortunate peers, I seemed to have been dealt a gilded hand. And then it just got better.

During my final weeks at school a friend had invited me to go to a photo shoot in London for an

Italian magazine. The photographer was apparently casting his feature from the pretty boys who could at the time be found lounging around the streets of Chelsea. I went to this bizarre event and actually enjoyed myself. The photographer had a knack of putting us at our ease. He was Mario Testino, who turned out to be one of the most famous photographers of our generation, and Lady Diana's favourite. I can understand why. In quick order he put me on the cover of an Italian magazine and by the time I returned from my family's summer holiday in Sardinia, I was signed up with London's top modelling agency. So I started my 'gap year' with no fixed plans but with an international invitation to pocket-money, parties and glamour. Really you couldn't make it up.

I arrived at Oxford University as a freshman, worldly wise, having travelled and met an extraordinary cross section of people, from a princess to the son of a Peruvian miner and everyone in-between through this very paradoxical pastime of male modelling. It was the best possible antidote to an Eton education because the fashion industry was blind to background. The only thing that mattered was the surface. I had about £10,000 of my own earned money in my student bank account, an almost unheard-of fortune for a student. It meant I could do anything I liked around town and run a car, and it bestowed upon me a sense that life was something that was just handed to me as required. Perhaps not the best preparation for getting on with the self-directed learning of university life.

So I had perhaps the most explosive, dangerous, unstable and delusional of all possible starts in life. I had been by any standards an extremely worried and traumatised child from perhaps as young as four months, when my mother was diagnosed, to the time of my settling with my father in his new family at their new home around the age of two. Psychologists will talk about years zero to three being the 'psychological birth' of the child. If you get these years right, most of what follows can usually be coped with, good or bad. Get them wrong and you risk permanent damage to the brain, which makes everything that follows much more difficult. (Studies of orphans in Romania tragically showed that babies who had suffered a total lack of physical affection were missing actual parts of their brains.)

On top of this damaged early development was layered a rich, societal delusion. The same swagger, pomp and circumstance that allows the British Prime Minister (at the time of writing) convincingly to convey that he has some right and entitlement to run a whole country, was given to me through the very same system of expensive schools, elite university and peer feedback. I was the best of the best and seemingly nothing was beyond my grasp or reach. The fantasy was that whatever path I took in life, it would lay itself out for me like an open run towards a Shangri-La horizon. Where others, even my friends and school-boy peers, struggled to get a toe-hold in the citadels of good fortune, I was merely breezing through open doors. People who knew me at the time would most likely have resented me as somewhat aloof and arrogant, which was true but not because I was pleased with myself, instead because deep down I was afraid of them. I could also be very charming and kind or generous too, never missing an opportunity to

11

invite a friend to enjoy something at my expense. I was, in an uncomplicated way, naturally generous, but maybe underneath that it was a strategy to find a way to be with people. I found it hard to connect with people but survived through achievements, success and status.

You might wonder how this turned out, and really that's where this story starts. In the summer of 2008 I was beginning to drop the spinning plates which held me in place. Throughout my twenties and thirties, I had had to make life up as best I could. I had been to film school in Los Angeles, run a nightclub business in Soho in London, was one of Tatler's most eligible bachelors and, after getting married and having children, I tried to escalate my business activities to match my burgeoning overheads. I was allegedly 'close' to my original family but in reality we were satellites to each other, islands in a loose archipelago.

Looking back now, I can see that I was plagued by an anxiety disorder throughout this time which made the normal activity of life hard to bear. I never really went anywhere without my wife; I could not hold down a normal job for long; I withdrew from friends and many social activities. During a crisis phase of panic attacks, triggered by the end of a long relationship in my late twenties, I decided to get a 'proper job' as my grandmother had called it. I applied for a position at Goldman Sachs, possibly the hardest normal job available to get in London, and got it. I was unable to take it up because it meant five weeks training in New York and I couldn't face the panic attacks. So I invented a parallel reality, one in which I could live like a banker and yet still behave like a child. That dubious solution worked for both

parts of me, but required some re
in order for me to sustain it.

Some of the edifice that pro'
way of life had some substan.
successful-ish young entrepreneur in
which gave me the capital to buy a house in .
Grove when I got married and start family in.
some style.

During a summer hiatus from the entrepreneurial
life, I had taken a foundation course in psychotherapy
and discovered a certain unexpected gift for the work,
which brought me a lot of joy intellectually and
emotionally, but seemed to lack any reasonable
prospect of bringing in the type of income to which I
had so fatally grown accustomed. On that same
course I met Dorothea and we became inseparable.
So it was that I was handed two new starts – one in
my career and the other in my personal life – both of
which came with their own financial challenges.

Somehow the media found me and I was then able
to combine my teenage experience in front of the
camera with my new found psychological talents in a
long-running BBC series started in 2004 on the
psychology of money and how people spend it.
During the four years of filming Spendaholics on and
off, I fell into a new layer of fantasy, a delusion that
somehow the magic of television would allow me to
pay for the only life I knew and also enable me to
work as a psychotherapist. I was wrong.

Television is an exploitative industry at best and, in
the reality shows, it is not at its best at all. It sucked
me in and spat me out like everyone else, entirely at
my own volition, fuelled only by a few vague
promises of more shows, a larger audience and some

success. While I was waiting for it all to come
good, I was funding my life in an increasingly
desperate cycle of unsustainable manoeuvres.
Ironically, these were exactly the kind of things which
we were exposing on the television programme. I
remember that we would be recording the head of a
programme with some castigated volunteer, gasping
at his or her £20,000 debt, whilst I myself had a
mortgage of many times that and rising, (not least
because I made my interest payments by increasing it
all the time). It is perhaps why I was very good on the
programme: I knew straightaway exactly what these
people were feeling and why they were doing. They
were a mirror of myself, and I too was feeling terrified
and out of control.

By the time that summer came around, I was
running out of leverage, but still had enough
fantastical schemes in the pipeline to suggest to
myself the possibility of it all turning out ok. My
strategy had been to continue to use my
entrepreneurial and business skills while practicing as
a psychotherapist in my day job. This wasn't in itself
the worst idea ever. Psychotherapy is a poor relation
of the medical and scientific professions and most
people who work in it cling to the edge of starvation.
That may be because some of them are not very
good, but it is also a consequence of the way that the
industry is (or isn't) funded and these two factors may
indeed influence each other. The problem was that I
was engaged in a delusional world of make believe in
both spheres. This was a symptom of deeper
problems yet to be revealed, but also a dangerous flaw
in the hands of someone so superficially capable.

I had entered into some property deals in Greece,

having met some characters in that business through travelling there with my wife, who was Greek. It was 2007 and it seemed like domestic Greek property was about to go through the sort of value bubble which we had seen in the UK in the eighties, much like Spain and other territories had seen recently at the time. The driver was the relatively new availability of debt. Historically Greeks had owned their land and built on it, so the cost of homes was usually borne by the senior generation passing down some bricks and mortar to the newlyweds, who would spend their entire life in that family plot. This was in effect a mortgage in reverse: you would work your whole life and save money to buy your children a house, and they would do the same. With the advent of the EU, and particularly the Euro, Greek banking went through a step change into the modern era. Where previously debt had been at unstable interest rates rising into the high teens at the blink of an eye, there was now a real straightforward mortgage industry begging to sell the Greek nation on the hard drug of cheap, accessible debt. A nation of savers was introduced to the drugs of the northern European countries and the consequences seemed entirely predictable.

From my work on Spendaholics, I thought that I knew what would happen next. Everyone would borrow up to the eyeballs, buy homes that they could not otherwise afford, and so the price of these properties would escalate sharply leaving the developers who fuelled this bubble to make out like bandits before it burst. I had missed the latest bubble in London, having had to sell my house when the mortgage became exhausted, and so I thought this was my chance to get back into the financial territory which I believed was my birth-right. I was simply better informed in a niche market and therefore money owed me a living, once again.

So plausible was this idea that I managed to persuade my father to help me borrow money to execute it. We had a house in Greece which had become worth quite a bit, and my pitch to him was that he would help us to raise a fund against the value of that house. Greek borrowing was not sophisticated enough to provide debt against a house to someone with no income, so he kindly arranged for his bank to provide the facility against his own personal guarantee, which itself would be underwritten by the value of our house.

These were the days when money was a commodity which would never run out. The end of that era had not yet come and my father, and others, were themselves swimming in the idea that things could only get better. He himself was involved in some fantastical schemes. He had at least two seven-figure investments in rather opaque foreign escapades, and had been promised highly exciting returns from them both. So the idea of underwriting a large bank facility to build new homes with a local house builder in rural Greece seemed plausible enough. Honestly, what could go wrong? The money was being used to build houses, and that money itself was secured by the value of our house.

This may sound like a normal way for a father and son to interact about business, but it wasn't. There were so many layers to this transaction, layers of which I wasn't even aware myself until much, much later. Ancient myth is rich with the stories of fathers and sons, a special relationship which holds great power, both to create and to destroy. The stories of Icarus, who flew too close to the sun; Paris and Hector, two sons of King Priam of Troy, one of whom brought him honour and the other catastrophe; and Oedipus, who unwittingly killed his own father, bear witness to both the passions and the high stakes that this all-male intergenerational dyad can create. From father to son passes a baton of primal power and control, rich with symbolism and ancient archetype. When that succession doesn't pass easily, these themes of attention, sabotage and revenge can get stoked into high drama. In our modern world, money often becomes the currency of these male relationships. For myself and my father it seems that it may have been no different. I had no idea, at that time, why, but it locked us into a spiral from which neither of us would emerge unscathed.

As it turned out the arrangement was as disaster. Greek property in the summer of 2008 was probably one of the worst investments of all time, particularly for a foreigner. In a previous book What's Wrong With You? I posited the idea that on an unconscious level we may actually know everything about everything (this is a hypothesis, not a proven idea, but going with it is interesting). If this was the case, then it would suggest that both my father and I unconsciously collaborated in an arrangement which would end up with my being literally ruined and having a good go at taking him down with me. Why would we do such a thing? Even without perfect unconscious foresight, this seemed like a slightly unbalanced arrangement. Too much money was at stake and I knew too little about what it was I was trying to do, something about which my increasingly angry half-brother – who actually did know about foreign property – grew more and more restless to remind me. So on every level, there were reasons not to do this. The question therefore arises, how did it happen?

If you want to make my father happy, there are two very easy ways to do so. One is to make money and the other is to be good at cricket. I had attempted both. I was actually quite successful at cricket and played once for Oxford University (he, his father and his grandfather had all played regularly for Oxford, so I wasn't quite up to scratch). However, I have only ever broken two bones in my body, both in my fingers, and both while playing cricket in the Oxford University Parks. On sequential seasons, I had half a chance of becoming a regular university player, something which would have met his ambition for me to play cricket against the occasional visiting professional teams. In fact, in each case, this possibility was taken away from me by a rare injury, something unique in my long history of sporting engagements since a very young age. I remember even then thinking this was odd, that I had somehow found my way to injury just at the point when I was most likely to achieve his one burning ambition for me. It was almost as if I was doing it on purpose to hurt him.

With money, too, I showed some early promise. I am a natural, perhaps even gifted, salesman. With his knowledge behind me, I was comfortable with entrepreneurial activity. In my twenties I made money running a night-club business. By any standards I was an up-and-coming businessman of my generation.

Certainly by thirty I knew more about how to operate in this sphere than many people twice my age because I had the experience and the pedigree. I had bought my own five bedroom house in London and started family life without need, or request, for any contribution from my parents, which was becoming more and more unusual for my generation. I seemed to be on my way. Somehow, over the next decade, I seemed to contrive to turn all that to dust. By the time the global financial crisis of 2008 hit in early autumn, I appeared to wake up to the reality that I owed more money than I could ever hope to make through honest work and had virtually no chance of recovering any value at all against the assets I had bought with it. It perhaps took a few months for this reality to sink in, the prospects for selling anything in Greece just getting worse and worse as time went by.

But in retrospect it was a remarkable trajectory. I went from being an entirely self-made millionaire at thirty, to being all washed up at forty, with nothing to my name but a short list of very deep debts, many of which ultimately cost my father a huge sum of money against his personal guarantee.

I began to wonder what metaphor this narrative might be carrying. Going back further than Greek myth, I seemed to be acting out the original father-son fable of the prodigal son. I had wasted his inheritance to me, while my half-brother's good behaviour – he really was, as my father once described him, 'the perfect son' – went unrewarded. I was a bit like that character in the bible, eventually reliant on state help to feed and house my family. In my desperation I returned to him, asking, even eventually begging for help. How, and, more bafflingly, why, did I get there?

My own construction of my relationship with my father was simply that he was great and that I loved him very much. I loved his swagger in business, the stories he would tell, his explanations of how to get rich in life. I admired his sporting success, went regularly as a child to watch him playing cricket at a very high amateur level. And I hung on to his presence in the house, desperately craving that feeling of being close to someone to whom I was properly related. My step-mother and I never really clicked, and so when he was around, I suppose I felt more normal. He was that unique thing: someone from my very own tribe. In every way I wanted to be just like him. I, too, wanted to do well at cricket and to make money. These things seemed like fun, but they were also what I could tell he wanted. Part of the legacy of his success was that he was busy with his work. He would routinely put in twelve hour days at his company, usually the first to arrive and the last to leave. So I suppose it was inevitable, like many children in the modern era with successful fathers, that I didn't get to be around him as much as I might have liked.

But the overall feeling was one of great security and love in his presence. I remember his 50th birthday party, a very lavish affair in Highclere Castle (now the television set for Downton Abbey) for a hundred or so of his closest friends, during which he gave a speech thanking me for my friendship. I was so proud. As a young man, he seemed to me to be the ideal paternal role model, a man I would describe myself as close to and loving. What possible reason could I have for sabotaging that?

It is easy to see what's not wrong with any given relationship. We are predisposed, as children, to look for safety. Inevitably we find that in our parents, or their substitutes. In fact it is vital for the integrity and functioning of our nervous system that we do find a point of safety in a world which otherwise could overwhelm us with threat. Our capacity to survive as very young mammals without the support of a protective parent figure is zero. Humans are not born ready. We appear long before we can take care of ourselves in any meaningful way. Our brains take about three years to develop after birth; we can't move about or communicate; our social functions are extensively limited; we can't flee or defend ourselves; we can't gather even the most basic of resources; we are utterly dependent on the benign will of our caregivers.

In my case it was particularly important that my father became a safe haven. He was literally my only surviving direct relative from my family of origin, and it seemed that he could become the one point of close familial connection to endure into my developing life once we had reconnected in his second family. This connection, I would speculate, was important enough to me to defend against anything, any contradictory evidence. And yet we had drifted apart in adult life, in the seemingly normal separation that families go through as their children emerge into adulthood, ultimately finding ourselves on the wrong end of a disastrous business arrangement, perhaps designed in part to bring us closer together.

What was it that I was not seeing about our relationship? What was it that I had had to bury in order to make him that one consistent, immutable, permanent point of safety in my life?

It is possible that I was just a lazy, feckless product of a spoon fed educational system and a privileged background. Spoilt, if you like. My father was a self-made man, albeit with a good education, but someone who had taken care of himself. I was perhaps a poster boy for someone who had had it all handed to him on a plate. Perhaps I lacked backbone? Naval gazing about my relationship with my father, as if this episode meant something, could just be a distraction from the hard reality that I had been a fool; and that he had tried to help me; that I was a fraction of the man that he would ever be; that I thought life owed me a living and he had been my meal ticket. This might be a popular view in some sections of society. The habit of the unfortunate to find someone to blame is unpalatable. It is a very North American cultural norm to take on the idea that everyone has the same chance and that those who blow it have no-one but themselves to blame. In the chance stakes of life, I'd had a better start that anyone could imagine. If things had gone wrong, why would I need to look further than simply to my own character defects, or my own bad choices? It is a reasonable question, after all.

For me, even in the emerging dark tunnel of the nervous breakdown which was to follow this more superficial financial breakdown, there seemed to be a clear strand of meaning beyond this easy outcome analysis. I had been more financially independent of my parents from leaving school than anyone else I knew. I had made my own money and made my own choices. I had even paid for myself to go through graduate school in film production in Los Angeles at the age of twenty-one from money I had made in my first business. I was an early example of entrepreneurial zeal and prized my success and independence greatly. I believe that this made my father proud, although sometimes I even detected a faint whiff of envy, probably just a benign consequence of his fiercely competitive nature. Somehow this dynamic began to reverse as I entered into my own family life of marriage and fatherhood. Interestingly this was perhaps the exact opposite of many of my contemporaries, who would gratefully lean on some family support to survive their twenties and to set up a home of their own, and then move on to self-sufficiency in more reliable careers. I just seemed to hit a wall when my own family started. Looking back on it, perhaps I just wasn't ready.

My wife and I had only known each other for about five months when she became pregnant. I had told myself from our first meetings during that summer course on psychotherapy that I wanted to spend the rest of my life with her, so this wasn't itself particularly a problem in terms of the question it asked about our union. But it was nonetheless a big shock to a twenty-eight year old struggling to move on from a rather Peter Pan relationship with work, self and society. I had flourished by engaging in the things which I thought were fun – nightclubs, restaurants, the film industry – and had had a good run.

Now I was confronted with a whole new generational dynamic, that of becoming a father myself. With a good role model for a father, it seemed that this would be relatively easy, but somehow it just wasn't. The more that life was asking the big questions of me, the more I seemed to become a child again.

During my wife's first pregnancy I was a complete nervous wreck, utterly convinced that she would die in childbirth, something I later came to understand quite clearly in how it related to my own birth and my mother's subsequent terminal illness. Even though I became someone who frequently couldn't get out of bed, let alone the building, somehow I managed to set up a new company which provided for us to a certain extent, but it was all short-term, smash-and-grab type work. The idea of setting down permanent roots, settling, laying the foundations for a secure family life, all seemed to evade my completely out-of-control nervous system. I was plagued by anxiety, constantly overwhelmed, and looking everywhere and anywhere for relief. As much as I was overjoyed by my new child, there was something which this experience had stirred in me which was taking me backward, not forwards in life. Becoming the father was making me a baby again myself.

We went on to have three more children and during this time I would rouse myself to some semblance of normal fathering and then again fall into a trough of inaction and inability. I was clever enough to get away with it for quite some time, but in the end I found myself, through the autumn and winter of 2008 and 2009, more and more desperately appealing to my father to help me. I was entering into a period of profound mental ill-health, triggered by the quite reasonable concern of having no money, no job, not much by way of a career and huge debts. Onto the bonfire of these anxieties was poured the petrol of the surprise package of my wife's unplanned fifth pregnancy, announcing itself in the autumn of 2008, just as the world's economic markets hit their terminal moment.

What I began to notice was that whatever idea I had about how we could stabilise our situation, my father's input or help was never enough. He would engage with the problem, but I never felt comforted by his help. It always seemed to underestimate the scale of the problem, and the scale of my internal reaction to it. He was responding to external practicalities, whereas I was lost in the landscape of the infinite needs of my emotional world. I would always find myself ruminating over and over on what other argument could be made, what other angle could be taken, how I could elicit his help in other ways. It began to feel like a more insidious dynamic than simply that I was rather desperate and he was rather rich. Perhaps I had been building up to this all along? Certainly it threw us both closer together, literally giving us more reason to communicate and to spend time together, in a way which had been missing for the best part of a decade.

It would be a long, long time before I gained any insight into this dynamic. For now, the best that I could do was to bring a fragile corner of my awareness to the fact that something, beyond the screaming obvious, was not quite right about what we were doing. There was more to this story, layers yet to be revealed. But what was staggeringly apparent in the present was the florid malfunction both of my thinking and, more importantly perhaps, of my behaviour.

There is a therapeutic construct of the idea of the King Baby. This is a person who somehow combines the best and the worst attributes of both the king and the baby. On his best day, he can be both majestic and sublimely charming, something which I can relate to when things in my life were going well. The flip side of course is a dangerously out-of-control infantile need, manifest with the might and entitlement of some kind of royal decree. This latter part was where I had ended up. This is in itself an interesting conjunction: on the one hand magnificently overblown, and on the other childishly collapsed. These are two opposing sides of our reaction to difficulties in childhood, sometimes called the wounded child, helpless against the weight of what is done to him or her; and the adapted child, eventually rebelling against this earlier injustice. I had lived an 'adapted' life, but now it had pancaked on top of me and I had nothing left but my 'wounded' self.

As the autumn of 2008 rolled through the global financial crisis, I was at the absolute summit of both of these inauthentic positions. I had lost touch with any semblance of reality and probably reached this point by being completely absent from my true self. The consequences for the people around me and for those who depended on me seemed to be catastrophic. I had built a financial pyramid for myself, with ever increasing stakes, predicated on the magical thinking that everything would turn out ok because it always had done in the past. My father was entangled in a Greek debt mountain and, in addition, I had entered into a contract to buy a very expensive house in Oxfordshire, which was now going to be impossible to complete on. I had various debts outstanding left right and centre, and no viable way to take care of my family. My response to this was to collapse, to regress to the condition of a baby, and to fall on my father to take care of me. Neither position of course is healthy. Neither is an adult presentation. Neither makes any sense from afar.

From the end of 2008 until the end of 2013, my work, both personally and professionally was to make sense of this insanity, which on the face of it was a Herculean task. What I learned was the true depth of human suffering from mental ill-health; the possibility of healthy human behaviour; the behavioural dynamic of unresolved trauma, first in the physical anatomy of my own nervous system, then in the detritus of my acting-out behaviour, and finally in the attachment disorders of my relationships which perpetuate our suffering through generations of trouble.

Most unhappily though, what I also learned was the terrible truth, the denial of which had been the cornerstone of this surreal fantasy which had become my life. It was the darkest part of our most shameful, most buried and most disowned history, and therefore the part of myself which was going to be the most brutal to recover.

2 BREAKDOWN

During the early autumn of 2008 it became very clear that the external circumstances of my life were not going well. My wife was pregnant with our fifth child. I had no income, very little work and to a certain extent no real career. I was absurdly in debt and the assets which supported this debt were plunging to almost negligible value due to the global economic collapse and their own particular position within that, in Greece. I had three children in private schools who had just started a new academic year and was renting an expensive house in London. I had been living like a millionaire for about a decade, and had become accustomed to this way of life. I had a few quid left in the bank and no idea what would happen next. At thirty-nine, it seemed to me that my life was over, just as it appeared to be beginning in earnest for my contemporaries.

The first thing that I noticed of course was the worry. There were a lot of practical things to be concerned about. Almost everything in fact: housing, education, work, income. Most of the basic elements needed to sustain and support a family were up in the air. I had always lived somewhat on my wits and at the edge of what perhaps a 'normal' person would consider to be wise, so I was comfortable with a certain amount of risk and unpredictability. But I had tipped this balance way, way too far and was beginning to experience what it was like to go over the edge.

At first I just started to try to solve the problems. They seemed innumerable and my internal capacity for bringing my normal problem-solving self to them wavered. Part of the difficulty was that the world itself seemed to be so out of control. During October 2008 wave after wave of financial Armageddon swept over the news and media. I would try to steady myself against the new reversals, thinking that now I could start to make a plan to recover from this position, but then further bad news would arrive, shattering my confidence in a general recovery, let alone in my own. I had sailed into the worst financial shock in a century with my own personal financial position as fragile and as leveraged as it had ever been. The timing was exquisite. If I had been trying to make things as bad for myself as they could have possibly been, I probably would not have been able to come up with a scenario this effective. Everywhere I turned, my life was crashing into dust. The scale of the task ahead of me simply seemed to be too much.

I could get obsessive with worry anyway at the best of times about small issues, but now I began to notice that the habit of worrying was getting out of control. I really couldn't do much at all with my brain except go over my problems time and time again. I exhausted my wife, family and friends with my neurotic anxieties. My thinking would go round and round, and just when I reached any sense of resolution with one theme, I discovered dozens more problems queuing up behind each requiring urgent solutions. There were the very fundamental threats of nowhere to live, no schools for our children, no food for the table. And then we had posh problems, like just getting used to not having a cleaner in a large house with four – nearly five – children and having to look at what we could sell or do without. We had some big adjusting to do. The practical challenge of learning to live with less was probably just an ordinary difficulty, and survivable. My wife, after all, had grown up with very little in a working-class Greek family. But for me it threw up huge questions of ego and identity. I had been blessed with material abundance in my own life ever since leaving school and with surprisingly little effort expended to get there, it seemed. My father had been quite rich since I was a teenager. I very much did take my wealth and material success for granted. I faced a huge existential shock, apart from anything else, at seeing that this had been an illusion. I had believed that I could never run out of money, that somehow I had a Midas touch which would sustain me through odd decisions and baffling behaviour. I honestly believed that I was special and different, immune to the mundane requirements of self-care to which the rest of the world needed to bow. I was going to be alright, I thought. Looking back, I'm astonished and horrified that I could have ever thought like that. It was, I suppose, a defence against never really believing that I could live up to the life that I had been set up for.

A few of the bigger practical problems began to resolve themselves at least for the short term. My father helped us with a term's school fees and I discovered, somewhat to my amazement, that our landlord was willing to lower our rent. But these were temporary fixes merely. Unsurprisingly, these sticking plasters were inadequate in the face of the relentless downward spiral of my internal state of being. I realise in retrospect that I had begun a slow descent off a cliff into an abyss, which no half-decent intervention was going to arrest. Possibly if I had won £10m in the lottery, I would have stabilised, but then again maybe not. There were clearly much deeper processes at work.

In a way, this was what I had so long been avoiding. All my life I had been living as if this wasn't possible, staving it off my inevitable fall with a cavalier (to the point of deluded) attitude to the potential pitfalls. I had been on the run for a very, very long time from the core issues of myself, and now they were beginning to catch up with me, viciously, relentlessly. There was no effort I could make to outrun this now. It was like trying to accelerate to the speed of light – the faster you go, the more energy it requires to go any faster. I had run out of time.

I had discovered one prop during this time – a faith healer of whom I was fond and who I believed in. She had been recommended to me by a friend many years earlier and was clearly highly gifted. She had often helped me in the past, somehow making me feel calmer in myself and giving me seemingly psychic advice on how to life my life. I had no idea what she did, but whatever it was it always seemed to leave me feeling much lighter, more grounded and present. I would literally see more clearly after leaving her sessions, by which I mean that I could actually see colours and scenes more vividly before my eyes, kind of like waking up when already awake. During the sessions themselves, she would rarely touch me, but instead just wave her arms over me and around me, working it seemed systematically but nonetheless, to me at any rate, mysteriously. Sometimes I would feel something moving in my body, like heat or energy, but I never understood it, and she couldn't really explain it. She did however talk a lot about other things. She had a strong conviction in the complexity of our metaphysical universe, which included a panoply of gods and demons. She was comfortable with the art of magic, both black and white, and she was just as au fait with talking about the future as the past, as if they were both simply stories already written, waiting to be read. It was the future which of course particularly interested me.

I came to rely on my weekly visits to her in her comfortable home in North London as a straw of hope onto which I could cling. She would both make me feel better and, more importantly, tell me what was going to happen. My mantra throughout that whole autumn of tumultuous changes was, "What is going to happen to us?" To be with someone who seemed so confident that she knew gave me a moment's calm in that incessant storm. So in two important ways, she became a strong crutch to lean on. First, she actually made me feel physically less unwell, calmer and more settled in the moment, somehow in my body. Second, she pulled off the miraculous coup of making me worry less, at least for a few minutes about the future. As a result of this, I came to give her a very large slice of power and responsibility over my life, my decisions and my health. She didn't take this from me; it was my choice. She was a good and kind person, treating me for free when I was least able to afford her sessions. I have no doubt that she is a force for good in this world, but I'm not sure that my choice to defer my life to her was a wise one. I did it because I thought that she had a window into something, presumably something supernatural, which I lacked, and that through that window could be seen the real answers to my pressingly overwhelming and tumbling problems.

In a parallel way, I had also developed another raft to cling onto. During the early spring of 2008 I had been driving along behind a bus in Chiswick and noticed the advertisement on the back of it. It seemed to me that there was a word which was literally glowing and levitating out of the very fabric of the two-dimensional placard. The word was 'alpha'. Now, I have a very firm academic background in the scientific method, and I fancy myself as a pure and disciplined empiricist. This means that I am schooled in the necessity of gathering evidence before pronouncing on theory, so weird anomalies like this actually interest me.

I looked more closely. It was an advert for the Alpha course, which I discovered to my horror was a kind of slightly cultish introduction to Christianity for lay people and ditherers. Nonetheless, I just couldn't avert myself from this interesting connection. I became completely fascinated by the oddness and possible significance of what had happened to me behind that bus, what it might mean, and whether or not it had a place of importance in my life.

I had grown up from eight to eighteen in very English boarding schools. These were run on the vague premise of a Church of England establishment in the loosest sense. School assembly, up until the age of about sixteen, was in chapel, conducted against the backdrop of a very traditional piece of Christian worship, with old fashioned hymns and prayers. Sunday church was obligatory, and usually very, very boring. The vicars who I met did not distinguish themselves. The schools certainly did nothing to espouse Christian values, at least not that I could see. They were elitist bastions of privilege in which almost everything unpleasant that could be done or said went on routinely. So my experience of Christianity, or church, was almost religiously negative. Why on earth would I now choose to put myself in a room full of people who made it their business to promote such terrifying nonsense? Surely that would be a madness all of its own.

The problem was my addiction to the scientific method. My greatest interest in life, really, is in understanding things. Something had really happened behind that bus, something odd and inexplicable. If I didn't follow through on it then I wouldn't know if I was deluded in that moment or if it meant something. The alternative was to go down a much more popular line of thinking, which would go something like bus adverts can't glow, obviously, so I must have been losing my mind and therefore it means nothing. However, my experience, my empirical reality, was that something had really happened. I challenged myself to find out what.

Unfortunately for me, an Alpha course was just

about to start for the summer term, so I felt I had no choice but to go along, completely terrified, and put myself into the heart of something very alien and intimidating to me. Oddly, the experience was a revelation. It took me a few weeks to get over how strange everyone was and what they were doing, but the reality was that people were very nice to me, the exploration of Christian ideals and philosophy was genuinely interesting and, more importantly, I became aware of something else at work in that environment, something that perhaps could only be accurately described as supernatural. If pressed to put it in colloquial language, there seemed to be a kind of lightness of spirit about the way people went about their tasks there. They were perhaps 'spirited' in their enthusiasm for their mission, but of course, it was the 'Holy Spirit' which was credited with this catalyst of activity. For me, the idea that there could be anything remotely spiritual about church was a total revelation. I had always seen things which touched me in that way, such as yoga and meditation, as the antithesis of my childhood experiences in a boarding school chapel.

So I had two things going for me as my mind started to disintegrate, and actually both of them in different ways, despite very benign, well-meaning roots, were quite difficult, dangerous and probably destabilising to me in the condition that I was in at the time. Each had a notion of spirit attached to them – the spiritual healer, and the evangelical church soaked in Spirit. Both of them gave me a lift, equally in terms of my actual mood and my outlook on the future. Each time, this relief would wear off, and I would find myself craving it again, needing more, wanting it more often. I became enslaved to this idea that I could find a spiritual solution to my terrestrial problems. Framing my problems simply as a lack of money, there seemed to be hope that I too could benefit from the position taken by many in bible stories who have nothing, but nonetheless feel safe, happy and secure. I had glimpses of this condition of profound internal peace, but it would give way to more and more severe bouts of worry, stress and anxiety. If anything I think this rollercoaster was perhaps unhelpful. It suggested to me a possible exit route from the real channel of my suffering. This was perhaps illusory (barring an actual miracle) and so perhaps stopped me from pointing myself towards more grounded solutions, despite the incredible kindness and unselfish devotion given to me by those trying to help.

The real problem, though, and this is the nub of it, the reason for writing this book and the next two in this trilogy, is that the truth of what was really, happening to me was not known to me. It wasn't known to anyone I knew. It wasn't known to anyone to whom I turned for help. It was hardly known by anyone at all anywhere, and it would be a long, long time before I met up with someone who could explain it to me. In the meantime I became increasingly desperate, and in my desperation would turn to anyone and anything, any explanation, any idea, any plan, any solution. I was vulnerable, and started to regress into the ego state of the victim. As I did so, I set myself up to allow things to happen to me which I otherwise would never have tolerated. This is the condition of the person suffering from poor mental health. They need more and more help and, as they do so, they become easier and easier to exploit. Very rarely does anyone suffering in that position have either the knowledge or the strength to say "no". I was no exception.

Through the late autumn, I started to enter a phase of severe anxiety. I remember there was a point where I was worrying so much and so constantly that I thought that I would do some harm to my brain if I didn't stop. I was right. Gradually the process took me over. I started to feel it in my body. The anxiety went from a worry to a sensation physically shaking me. It would become a whole body experience. The tension, the palpations, the very speed of it, would be a constant presence in my system. I started to lose weight. Of course, I also began to look at how I could actually solve my problems too, but the tide was turning sharply against me. Partly I made this worse by the actions I took to rescue myself.

Clearly, since money was an issue, it seemed sensible to try to work as much as possible. I was actually a very well paid psychotherapist, when I worked, but had been keeping my face-to-face client work to a minimum for a few years because of my other interests and commitments. I had been working on and off in television and this mix seemed to work for me. Now the television work was over and I had the opportunity to start taking on regular clients. I had not previously held my clients over long periods of time, preferring to do consultations and to refer them on. It takes more out of a therapist to do regular work, so I was in the difficult position of pushing my psyche harder and harder at work to try to reverse the apparent superficial problem which was causing me so much worry. This unfortunately just accelerated my pace of degeneration. I was still able to work during the autumn, and sleeping fine, but my days were a tortured routine of endless looping thinking. It wasn't healthy and I couldn't sustain it for long.

I remember the Christmas of 2008. We had, from the remnants of our prior financial incarnation, a lovely house, a big fake tree, enough presents, food, four lovely children and a pregnant wife. All I did all day was shake. We had some friends over whom I had met at the church which I had continued to attend regularly, thinking I could pray away the anxiety like all the early Christians who seemed to positively beam with poverty. Although I could communicate with the simulation of superficial small-talk and sit with people, the only experience I could connect with was the one rampaging through my physical system. I remember my lower abdomen just trembling all the time. My body was just 'on'. I had probably lost two stone in the two months previously. I literally shook it off. I was still eating, as I did at Christmas lunch, but I must have been burning energy at such a rate that it was like starving myself despite the normal intake of calories.

It was interesting how I experienced these changes. I certainly didn't see myself then as I see myself now, looking back. That wasn't possible. Had I told myself then that I was sliding into a serious mental illness, then it would have made my worries even worse. Instead I rationalised that I was just taking on too many new clients at work and that 'their stuff' was overwhelming me. Partly this might have been true, but trying to solve the problem as if this had been all it was didn't work. I spent more time with my supervisor ostensibly discussing my clients, but gradually all we found ourselves discussing was me and how I was falling apart.

Then I stopped sleeping properly.

This is really when all semblance of normality began to leave my life, mind and body. Sleep, I have come to reflect, is a thing like money and love in as much as you can't really appreciate its value until you lose it. I began to wake up earlier and earlier in the morning, initially with a murmur, latterly with a start, then finally like a gunshot had exploded in my head. The worse it got, the more of an issue it became; the more of an issue it became, the more I worried about it; the more I worried, the less I slept. It got to the point where each morning I would wake up and the first thing I would do was look at my watch; then, seeing something like 3.15am, I would immediately panic that I was losing my capacity to function in the world, and the panic would untimely rip me wide awake. Then I would spend agonising hours in bed, trying to contain my tortured mind sufficiently to let me go back to sleep. I would budget an hour for a full-on worry attack, believing that this would then let me calm down enough to rest again. I didn't do anything helpful or constructive like get up or move around. I just lay there in the dark wrestling with my mind, thinking that this time I might get somewhere. Never, ever, did it work. Relentlessly I continued to try. Why? Why would I fall over and over again into the same hole? I had no idea what else to do. I couldn't properly understand what was wrong with me. My therapeutic resources seemed unable to solve this problem, the mind seeming to be so far away from the body where I was feeling this. And although I read lots of books and there was advice aplenty, I needed action, and short of medication, which I was loath to engage with the psy- professions seemed to have little to offer the severity of my condition. I wasn't able to fully look, honestly, at how ill I was and I had no idea what to do about the problem if I did. I was relying on the only resources I had: prayer and my spiritual healer.

The former was nice and comforting, if unproductive, but the latter started to go to places which, looking back on it, took me spiralling into some very murky territory, hurtling towards a dead end, via some very delusional thinking. But I was desperate. Someone who apparently knew what was going on and what to do meant everything to me, and that's what I thought my healer was. I had to believe that there was a way out. Otherwise the experience was just becoming too overwhelming.

Anxiety began to flourish into other, related, fragmented experiences. Bouts of depression would come over me in waves of severity. I became unable to countenance any kind of activity outside of the house. I reduced my work to a morning a week, and even this was becoming a stress of herculean proportions. Eviscerating emotions began to well up in me and press at the gates of my psyche, like tsunamis beating on a restraining harbour wall. Pressure built and built in my head but nothing would give way, nothing would pass. Into all of this my spiritual healer threw an interesting hypothesis, one which I was too weak to resist and desperate enough to cling onto. She had this idea that all of what I was experiencing was a resistance to coming through to a new level of consciousness. I had no idea what she was talking about, but it did often feel as if something

41

was trying to pass through my mind, body, system and that it was held at bay. The notion that this was something which could eventually just give way, like a dam finally bursting, was seductive. It meant that I was never too far away from a final resolution. She sold me on the idea that if I hung in there, and was willing to let go, there could be a sudden transformation into a new reality with much greater spiritual awareness, happiness and health. This was what I wanted to hear. So I stuck with my pain believing that it was somehow a royal road to some terminal relief.

I became an expert at suffering. I remember at one point driving down the a London street in the middle of the day, only able to be aware of the incredible emotional pain seemingly stuck in my head, unable to think freely, unable to plan, dream, converse, interact, fantasise, or even to complain; unable to do anything other than to be aware moment by moment of the fact of the agony which I was enduring. There was no other reality available to me. The totality of my capacity to notice anything was taken up with the experience of suffering from mental pain. I remember thinking, "Is this all my life is now?" I had nothing else happening to me, no other external or internal experience other than the nebulous and subjective experience of some kind of extreme mental distress. I could still drive, but I couldn't live. Describing it is like trying to translate the phenomenon into a language which has yet to exist. I can really only write around it, not through it; the actual experience itself is probably most clearly defined by being non-verbal and so it yields very reluctantly to the written word.

I remember such swings of emotional vicissitude

that I would actually gasp for breath as I tried to pass the time in these unending moments of all-encompassing pain. I would experience horror, rage, envy, despair, fear, shame, guilt in such torrential floods of pure emotion that I thought my system would simply give way. Instead it just ploughed on. During this phase of my developing illness, I could do nothing useful with my life. I could perform the basics of manual labour, but not hold any meaningful conversations. I was unable to interact meaningfully with my children, and was later described by my oldest daughter as a 'ghost'. I would simply follow my wife on her routine of the school run and caring for our home and children. I therefore found myself a passenger on a child's weekly schedule, dragging my stressed self into all the least appropriate places for such an unwell soul. I remember all too well being at a child's play zone, watching as my wife supervised our daughter, clinging to my sanity as they did so. All around me the wheels on the bus were going round and round, but in my mind I was simply trying to hold on to the idea that I must survive this experience ten seconds at a time. I would just stand there, rocking gently, hoping no-one would really notice me. The pain was so strong, like a pressure hose forced into the back of my skull, and the experience of withstanding it so intense, that time almost stopped. I became aware only of my own mind and the next few seconds on the clock. I knew that I could make it through a few seconds more, and then a few more, and then a few more. If I kept it simple, I could survive.

Without a shadow of doubt, during these episodes, if someone had put a loaded gun into my hand I would have put it to my head and pulled the trigger instantly. It sounds dramatic to say so now, but at the time it would simply have been a normal response to an overwhelming need for effective relief from my suffering. It's no different in my mind now, looking back on it, to taking a Nurofen when I have a headache. I'm grateful that I didn't own a gun at that time and that I maintained just about enough presence of mind not actively to seek one out, but if one had been given to me, there is absolutely no doubt about what I would have done with it, instantly. The imprisonment of suffering was complete, total and immense. The deluge of emotion was breaking me in two.

My symptoms seemed to mature along with my wife's pregnancy. Sometime in her third trimester I started to develop intense screaming fits. These would begin with my normal feeling of emotional overload, which would build and build into an internal sensation flooding the whole mind and body with a relentless sense of bursting mental agony. I couldn't sit still, I couldn't talk, I couldn't interact in any way. Every moment was taken up with the very immediate torture. Anything outside of that, even basic pleasures like reading a newspaper or cooking a meal, was simply a parallel universe which I could see being enjoyed by others, but to which I could no longer relate. I remember my last professional assignment was to do a photo-shoot for Psychologies magazine, for which I did a regular monthly consultation with a reader. I had to do this shoot every three months or so, and since the previous one, I had deteriorated massively. It was important to me to try to keep this work, but the shoot was a nightmare.

My mind was simply bursting. I sat with people who had come to me for help a few months previously, with a camera crew joking around, editors busying themselves with shop talk and gossip, and I could not maintain even a normal disposition. I was exploding and my only relief was to get up and walk round and round the garden, like a manic toddler self-soothing. I could hardly talk and surely they must have noticed that I was barely functioning, but nothing was said. My main preoccupation was to contain myself so that I didn't explode right there in the room. I was, after all, there because I was a professional mental health expert, supposed to be able to look after these readers. I somehow stumbled myself through the day, clamping down on my agony, until I was released to the haven of my car. Once safely in it, I gave way to that screaming fit, sitting as I was in a cold Mini on a north London suburban street. I brought myself back to some kind of sanity by screaming, a kind of primal howl of disturbance and distress, finally unobserved in this empty suburban street.

This was something which had crept up on me. At first I found myself doing it at home into a pillow. I thought I could get away with it, not wishing either to worry or to annoy my wife too much. Unfortunately, even with a pillow, the sound of a full-bloodied male scream tends to get around a small house. She would come and check on me, sometimes concerned, sometimes frankly exhausted. I remember well kneeling in front of her and wailing into her large, pregnant belly. She just looked at me, kind of resigned, impassive. I think her own experience of bouts of depression allowed her to think that this was

45

simply something I would recover from in time, and she seemed patient. For the children I think it was less straight-forward.

There was a time I remember being curled up on the bathroom floor in floods of screaming tears, and looking up to see my oldest two children in the door. My wife was there too. Astonishingly, we tried to normalise this, telling them that I was upset about my mother who died when I was a baby. I think we all, including the children, pretended that they believed us. Through all of this I somehow held onto a fantasy that I was in some important way OK. I had completely gone with the idea that these were simply some finite list of experiences which I had to process and, that having done so, I would emerge into a nirvana of being my normal self again. I absolutely could not engage with how ill I was. I think in retrospect it would have been impossible to have known that I was that ill, to have had no idea what to do about it, and to have had to accept it. It would just have been too terrifying. I was having therapy, going to church, and having healing. One or other or all of these were surely supposed to work in the end. It wasn't getting me anywhere close, but I didn't dare to see that for myself.

Weirdly, and perhaps unhelpfully, after a full-blown, dam-bursting screaming fit, I tended to feel all right for a few hours, almost back to something like normality. I would be calm, I could make sense in a conversation, I had a much less severe sense of my symptoms. Even so, I would still have to be very careful what I exposed myself to. Stressful situations such as dealing with financial problems or a conflict in the family could trigger distress again all too easily.

Unfortunately, the fleeting glimpses of my old self fuelled my fantasy that the suffering was simply a residue of some kind of childhood experience which was working its way, helpfully, through my system. It would be a long time before I was educated in a more expert understanding of this dynamic, so for the meantime, I gave myself to exploring these stresses, their screaming outbursts, and the moments of tranquillity which followed them. The problem was that the intensity, the experience, the frequency and the volatility of this stress was increasing and, as it did so, I was beginning to become mentally and physically even more drained.

Not sleeping was a massive problem. Continuing worries about money and work were omnipresent. Plus I really had nothing to do. I had had to give up working completely, and suddenly, and we were living off a dwindling supply of the odd tatty pocket of savings. Almost any engagement with the outside world was overwhelming. I couldn't watch television without being triggered into a state of panic by almost anything. Reading the paper was a nightmare; emails were just too painful. Even driving around town was too much. I would see an estate agent's sign on a house and become flooded with the despair of never being able to have a home of my own again. I would see the writing on the side of a van and collapse about the fact that there was a productive business and I could never now run one. Nothing was safe. Everywhere I looked, every single strand and evidence of ordinary lives grinding on relentlessly reminded me of what I had lost and of what I was convinced I would never have again. And in the state I was in, that was a fairly safe bet. On top of becoming really very ill, I began to feel very sorry for myself too, a bad combination.

My days stretched hopelessly before me, agonising metaphors for the empty life which also stretched before me, coming full circle to panic me in the moment. Any plan I might have had for recovering my life relied on the cooperation of my mind and body to be able to follow through with it, and yet really I was paralysed, either inert in a ball of frozen emotional pain, or screaming into a pillow, hiding in the bedroom. So I came up with a brilliant strategy. I would get a job.

The idea is a traditional one: that employment leads to many experiences which enhance mental health. It's a sound and well proven thesis in the realm of exploring life's less troubling difficulties, but employment as a treatment for severe mental illness was just another one of my desperate delusions, born out of a terrified confusion as I stumbled around the wilderness of my own mind. Everyone had an opinion; almost no-one knew what to do; but the instruction just to "get a job" seemed simple enough to follow. Very kindly an old friend offered to employ me to help with a project at his small company which he had built up over a decade. He had occasionally asked me for advice in the past. Now he was interested in developing the business in a new direction and thought I could possibly help. I suspect he knew that it was him helping me more than the other way round. What he wanted me to do would have been a simple enough task for me under normal conditions but, in the state I was in, it was a huge, awful challenge. I didn't have to do that much, but what I did have to do – reasonably enough – required travel, meetings, and some preparation. Alas, each one of these might as well have been the equivalent of an assault on Everest with nothing to support me but a bit of frayed rope and some old woolly gloves. In a way it is a remarkable testament to the human spirit that I was able even to attempt this work. Since there was an idea that it would help me to get well, I was willing to try to do it. In fact, I would try to do anything to stop the awful symptoms of my decomposing mind, crumbling under the weight of sleep deprivation, massive emotional swings and crushing psychological energy. I did what I could, and was able to make a contribution of sorts, but I was working at about ten per cent capacity and therefore really just abusing my position, abusing even my friend. This was something – exploiting loyal family and friends – that I later came to see as a lifelong problem[cut], but at the time I clutched at the straw generously offered by this particular friend so violently that had it been razor blades, and had my hands been bleeding relentlessly from every cut, I would have thought nothing of simply clinging tighter, and tighter and tighter until they ripped completely apart.

And then my wife went into labour.

Having already been through four births with her, the routine was fairly familiar. I just prayed that I could somehow gain enough relief from my symptoms to be able to be there for her, as opposed to the other way round, which was the sorry state of affairs that had dominated almost the entire term of her fifth pregnancy. I think, unsurprisingly, with so much stress in her life, the birth was not as easy as her previous ones. But I did just about manage. In a similar way that I had managed to do some work, I found I was able to push through my suffering for a few hours in order to be there for her during hers. It was an act of will, perhaps even of mercy. Seeing her for a few hours in a more dire state than I was gave me a small window of opportunity to be there – if briefly – for her for a change. Fortunately, I was even able to be quite useful, knowing her and her pregnancies as I did by then so well. She was able to overcome her most acute crisis and managed to have a natural, safe birth. We took David home that night and I had hoped that, with this obvious anxiety out of the way, there might be some improvement in my own condition. I was wrong.

Sitting still was torture for me. My mind was constantly in a pressure cooker of anxiety, emotion and depression. Even with a new baby in the house, I couldn't settle on any simple task to keep me grounded. I was unable to engage with doing anything meaningfully productive, and yet desperately unhappy when unoccupied. My wife was strong and impressive but the same could not have been said of myself. With the bank holiday weekend coming up, I thought that taking the whole family on a weekend to a caravan park on the South Coast would be a great way to try to recover from our recent troubles. One of the few things which made me feel slightly better was driving, and this was a good long car journey of several hours. So we packed up our family, with our new baby, and set off to an unknown holiday camp in Dorset. This probably wasn't such a great idea.

For me, rather than being the end of the beginning, as I had hoped, this turned out to be the beginning of the end. The drive did distract me, but the caravan park was a crowded, manic, busy place, full of families hoping for a long weekend of entertainment. The children were excited and desperate to do all the activities on offer, and I tried to anchor myself in helping them to keep busy and happy, but I was going downhill fast.

I remember walking around and around the caravan, wrestling with the stress and tension in my head. I suspect that the unfamiliar environment was making me feel worse. Again it was as if there was a pressure hose forced into the base of my skull and my whole being was occupied with the urgent business of managing my excruciating pain. I was still sold on the idea that this was something which just needed time to pass, that somehow this was a productive process which would result in some resolution, gloriously passing me up into a new phase of spiritual awareness and existence. So I brazenly faced it, grimly hanging onto the cliff edge of this awful mental sledgehammering, believing that the way out was through. My children were trying to play tennis with me, but I couldn't stand still for long enough to engage. I had to keep moving, nothing about being me was OK. It needed to avoid myself. I desperately needed help. Instead, I was on a budget holiday with my wife, her mother and five young children, including a new-born baby. On reflection, it seems like a madness in itself that we were there at all.

That night I visited a place inside me which I look back on and recognise as the true gates of madness. I was feeling worse than ever and wrestling with keeping my distress to myself, not to alarm my children or to burden my wife. I couldn't even get to sleep, let alone stay asleep. I lay in the dark, in a tiny unfamiliar bed, next to my sleeping wife and infant son, and I wrestled with the torrential forces in my mind. I would say that I didn't sleep at all, and not for one moment was I not busy. There appeared to open up before me a long, dark tunnel, like an abyss, or a vortex; a black hole beckoning me towards it. It was seductive. It offered the relief of total abandon. My whole sense of self hovered at the rim of it, flirting with the massive temptation simply to fling myself down, though, beyond, into a certain chaos, but one without the horror of the dreadful effort of resistance. The way ahead was clearly disastrous, but also possibly without guilt, responsibility, effort, or the need to recover, to survive, to provide for a family.

The way it seems to me, I must have spent hours during that night willing myself back from the brink. It was like trying to restrain a solid object from flying into a black hole. My mind had the force of a restraining rope, and my work was constantly, relentlessly to tug on it, not to allow the situation to slip any further towards the inevitable consequence of accelerating oblivion if it was able to pick up any speed towards the centre of this darkness. Somehow I held myself there. I'm not sure how, or even why. I think that the need to stay sane for my family was one aspect; the fear of this pitching into the blackness being a one-way journey was another; but to a certain extent it was just stubbornness.

All throughout this experience, I had a strong belief, like a sense of a truer self, that this was not the way that it was supposed to go, that this was not me, that I was living a parallel experience, outside of the one I was meant to have. The sheer bloody awfulness of what I was going through pissed me off. This anger, I think, kept me – relatively – sane.

I'm fairly sure that on the other side of that tempting void was a clean break with reality: madness, in the common sense of the word. I have a feeling that had I gone that way, a full recovery would have been a very distant, if impossible, task. In all of the severity of my symptoms, which in many ways really did amount to a losing of my mind, I never wholly let go of a sense of who I was, where and why. I have seen people who have crossed that line and I wondered about how that progression would happen. My own answer is that there is a threshold where pain is swapped for sanity; where the madness begins as an antidote to the totally bitterly, unbearable agony of mental chaos and mayhem. For me, the fight was still on, if in many ways only just beginning.

For the rest of the weekend, my mind was in a flat-out overdrive. Really any sensation, or definition of the holiday experience had ceased to be present. I was just flooded mental pressure. Perhaps screaming, or tears would have reduced it, but it was like a flat line of white noise. There seemed to be no longer any granularity about it, nothing to work with, no ebb and flow, nothing to inspire hope, to cling to, or to improve upon; just a constant chorus of fire alarms going off in my head, like an silent air-raid siren which never, ever ends. My experience had been that if I held on, this would pass, and so I did. I was numb with pain, rendered speechless. I could hold the baby, and that was all. I couldn't talk, play, help, participate. My family wandered the beaches of a gorgeous sunny Dorset day, and I paced back and forth, holding a baby, trying to hold on to myself. I knew that it would pass, but it didn't. A whole day of wall to wall agony, and little relief the next.

We were driving back via my cousin's house for lunch. On the way I felt something give. My fantasy was that I had now done it! The promises of my spiritual healer perhaps had been finally delivered. By holding firm, by letting it pass through me, by staying with the experience, perhaps I had finally processed my core pain, passed into a new realm. Certainly I was becoming much calmer. It was like a storm suddenly passing; stillness dawned upon my mind for the first time in days. I thought it was a miracle, perfectly timed for our visit – I had been dreading how I would explain to them that I couldn't sit still, or eat, or really even talk. As the children ate their lunch, I started to see the world very differently. Everything was clear, colours were brighter, faces were glowing, people were closer. I felt as if I was glimpsing this "other side" of which my spiritual guru had spoken. It was unnerving, but certainly could be blissful. Was it really possible that I had reached the end of my drama, a graduation from my suffering? I certainly was willing to believe so. It had been what I had been promised, and so desperately needed. After the weekend I'd had, I really didn't have any more fight left in me anyway.

So it was with some disappointment that I felt the old enemy of anxiety seeping back into my system on the drive home. I didn't want to credit it with any substance, or reality. I wrote it off to an echo, a residue. I was keen to get home and to get to sleep, to let the system settle, to reinforce my recovery. I woke with a terrified start in the middle of the night. It was like a giant gas bubble of fear had broken the surface of a molten tar pit. My mind exploded with terror, was enveloped in it. Nothing had been achieved.

Everything was still just as terrible as before. I had another round of mental wrestling to face for the hours ahead until dawn, and then another day to limp through in this disabled state. I simply couldn't face this fight again, any more. I had given my all that night in the caravan. I had nothing left. This new wall of emotion was like a tidal wave before an exhausted surfer. I threw my hands up and finally, desperately, reached out for some more conventional help, pitching me into an unknown world of even greater disturbance.

At breakfast that day I told my wife to call my parents and arrange for me to be admitted to a famous south London psychiatric hospital, assuming, as many do, that this was the best mental hospital in London, and that this would be the nuclear option to solve my problems. She was shocked, appalled even, disappointed in me. But I needed to go somewhere. I was becoming suicidal in my despair and could not even pretend any more to meet the demands of my growing family. And so I was trotted off to the fancy family doctor, and then to the gates of the London's poshest psychiatric hospital.

And that is when my real problems began.

3 TREATMENT

I arrived at this institution – a large, old, famous psychiatric hospital in South London – a shattered human being, barely able to communicate, my mind and self in multiple fragments. I had had to call my parents to come to the rescue to take me there. My wife was furious, seeing it as a weakness, possibly unable to bear to see quite how ill I really was. I was desperate though. I couldn't take another day or night of this suffering and recognised I was going to have to cross the Rubicon of taking drugs to get some help. I'd never met or talked to a psychiatrist before. Despite a career in mental health, I had not needed to. My view was that these drugs, such as anti-depressants, were a denial of the psychotherapeutic process and therefore an unhelpful alternative to what was really required. How I had formed this view, I am not really sure. I suppose that in therapy it becomes apparent that there are things which work and things which don't. I simply put drugs in the category of the latter and rather wrote them off. Now I felt as if I was dying and so was willing to try anything. Still, it was terrifying to engage with something new from a position of internal devastation.

It was immediately apparent that I had shifted into a different paradigm of treatment. I had stopped being one of the walking wounded, limping on with my life hoping it would all turn out ok, and had become a serious case, requiring a serious solution.

The first stage of the process of making it into hospital was to obtain a doctor's referral. My parents lived in a posh part of London and down the road from them was a very nice GP who had a private practice catering to the needs of mainly rich locals. On the day I could take it no longer, they were able to book an appointment for me to see her immediately and shepherded me into her practice. I had completely regressed: I was a thirty-nine year old man being led by my somewhat bemused elderly parents into the doctor's surgery, almost unable to walk let alone talk. I gratefully collapsed into the position of the child again, utterly relieved to be able to stop pretending that I could cope anymore – cope with my health, my life, myself, my obligations, my sanity. None of it was possible, not even a little bit, not any more. I wanted to be a baby again, just to be held and taken care of, and in this emotional place I stumbled into and was greeted by the most lovely and warmest of women, the perfect person I can imagine for listening to the complaints of well-endowed widows. But she and I, at that moment, were a massively incongruous pair. Her own health and happiness, obviously thriving in an upmarket medical practice, was almost tangible, and such a profound and awful contrast to my own devastated state in every conceivable way – personally, professionally and mentally. She referred me for admission to the hospital the following day and sent me home to my parents' house with a packet of Valium and something similar for sleep. And so it was I started medicating.

The drugs did calm me down a little, but made me feel very groggy and more depressed. I found myself retreating from my reality, and it felt as if my identity was disappearing down the plughole. In the morning they drove me to the hospital, a big, faded imposing building in south London. Even just approaching it in the car was overwhelming. This was the place where the rich and famous went into rehabilitation, but I was there (or so I perceived it) precisely because I had so completely failed to live up to either wealth or distinction. Things did not improve inside. The psychiatrists were all stationed in the most ornate part of the building, with a big waiting room and a team of secretaries buzzing around a large central area. My case was referred to the Medical Director. I was asked to wait and sat with my slightly over-awed parents wondering what on earth was to come. My father was still in shock at having had, on admission, a few thousand pounds gracefully lifted from his Amex card. I think in fairness we all shared the same bewilderment, in different ways, of having absolutely no idea what we were doing, or what was going to happen. But this was what posh people did when they had a breakdown, they check into this place, so we were surely doing the right thing. Alas, meeting the doctor didn't inspire much confidence.

He was an amiable Indian man, slightly short, but very well dressed. He showed us into his office, which was even bigger than the waiting room. He was delighted to meet my father, who was at that time the President of the MCC, an organisation which represents the interests of English cricket and runs Lords, England's home stadium for the sport. My doctor was a fan of the game and well aware of my father's position in the hierarchy of cricket's rather arcane and eccentric universe. This connection had a dispiriting effect on me. I immediately identified the doctor with my father, his world and his interests. My breakdown could perhaps in part be attributed to the consequences of my not having been able to become the man my father was. So having his aura infiltrating the very place, process and personnel of my treatment was not going to prove entirely beneficial. These were people who belonged to each other: members of the MCC, established professionals, successful men running respected organisations. I was just a piece of biological and financial detritus; broken and broke, worthless, waiting for the whim of their attention. Only in their own time did they eventually come round to the matter in hand, namely me.

I attempted to describe my condition. I went into my history and related my recent symptoms and experiences. I made a successful and complete presentation; so much so in fact that my father complimented me on it and asked the doctor if he was used to getting such articulate and fulsome accounts of his patients' troubles. The doctor listened patiently. At the end of my story, he had a view. First, he announced to my parents that the good news was that in psychiatry they now had evidence-based interventions both with drugs and in therapy which would preclude the need for messing around with the kind of therapy and ideas with which I was familiar. Second, he was able to offer me a diagnosis which would form the basis of my successful treatment and speedy recovery. Oddly, I didn't give a monkeys about him trashing my profession, once I heard his promise of recovery. There wasn't anything which I held so dear that I wouldn't have traded it at that point for some relief from the awful, hammering pain of my symptoms and the life in which it was trapping me. Whatever he was selling, I was buying. I did, though, have a million questions.

I was very, very worried about taking drugs and wanted to understand them. In fact I was so saturated with anxiety anyway that just reading an email would send me over the edge. Thus, even the thought of putting a toxic substance into my body was a grave concern. He was dismissive. His diagnosis was brilliant: "general anxiety disorder". At first I thought he was joking, because that was what I'd told him, that I was generally anxious. But he was sticking with it, if somewhat insecurely. I knew this because he offered to show my family that it was indeed a "proper diagnosis" by, in front of our very eyes, looking it up in a book! Regardless of the obvious emptiness of this label, his promise to me was that three weeks of medication would get me back to my old self. I was astonished. I had been falling apart for nine months; the idea that I could be literally my 'old self' in three weeks was transfixing, if a little hard to swallow. But I would have done anything for that. So I let go and simply gave myself over to his will. Quite sensibly, his first plan was to put me to sleep for five days.

After a painful admission process, endless

questions from new doctors and nurses and the horror of being left in my infantile state by my parents, I entered into a twilight world of heavy sedation. I remember nurses coming and giving me drugs, and noticed with astonished, grateful delight that within minutes I would find myself slipping into a powerful downward spiral towards sleep. I hadn't slept properly for nearly six months. This was a thing of wonder and delight. Three days drifted by without me. I remember a few fleeting moments of being woken in order for me to take my medication and then immediately passing back into sleep. It was heaven. But it couldn't last. Eventually they began to give me less sedation and I started to wake up. Of course I was very groggy, but did feel marginally better for the intervention. It was a double-edged sword though. There was no way I could live a normal life like this, stoned out of my mind, but when I asked for them to reduce the dosage, I returned to a highly anxious state, so much so that I had to ask for more sedation which required a call to my doctor who was on the golf course. It was the beginning of a new relationship for me, another nightmare: wrestling with medication.

I was very worried about everything and anything, so this just added to my concerns, not least because I swiftly discovered that I was highly sensitive to medication. It just didn't agree with me. Some people are like that. As a student, I had always had terrible hang-overs and couldn't drink for days after a session of doing so. I didn't like recreational drugs. Probably I was just generally too hyper-vigilant to changes in my body to cope with any interventions of this nature. When the doctor came to review my medication, I asked him a lot of questions. He was very sure that these questions were pointless but to me the reassuring answers I sought (but which were not forthcoming) were my only hope of calming down enough to cope with taking more pills. He was absolutely sure that some anti-depressants and CBT (Cognitive Behavioural Therapy) would fix me. I was even more sure that they wouldn't. He left my room on what must have been the third time I'd met him, his back to me, telling me that I was a "very difficult patient". And then he was gone, fleeing into the corridor, in his expensive suit and MCC tie. I was flabbergasted. As a therapist, I cannot offer people miracle cures in three weeks, but I do tend at the very least to be able to be polite to them. This incident left me with very little faith in his expensive hospital and his bespoke methods for my recovery.

I discharged myself after six days. All I was doing was sitting in the replica of a hotel room which happened to have a chemist in its foyer. I was told that my anti-depressants would take ten days to four weeks to kick in and in the meantime I would just have to wait. Most of the time even ten minutes was too long to wait, but I was sane enough to know that I could at least get through another few weeks of my inner hell if it meant a permanent escape from it on the other side. It seemed more sensible to acclimatise to the pills at home.

Unfortunately, in the more normalised and everyday context of home, I could see the severity of my condition reflected back to me more clearly than ever. My wife had just given birth to our fifth child and we were flat broke. I was unable to work, play or really even talk. I just took up a position on the sofa in front of the TV and set my mind to counting the days until the drugs would deliver their magic promise. Every moment was still agony but at least I had a new hope, even though I was all too aware of how redundant I had become, both at home and to the world. I was surrounded by the ever-increasing responsibilities that I now had as a husband and father and the huge gulf between them and what I could possibly provide. It was not ideal that, on top of all this, the drugs made me feel seriously weird.

I had hoped that the effects of my sedation would wear off, clearing my head, but no such luck. I was still taking sedatives while the other drugs were kicking in and the combination seemed to make me feel awful all of the time. When my anti-depressant dose increased, I began to find it impossible to get to sleep. This was a terrifying new problem. Before, I had at least managed to drop off even if I had been an early waker insomniac. Now, being unable to get to sleep in the first place meant I was entering a whole new realm of insomnia. Then I made a terrible mistake. I read the instructions. The list of side-effects of anti-depressants would make most sane people balk with terror. Perhaps it was a blessing I was not sane. Just desperate. And these pills were supposed to be my salvation. In the misguided quest for some comfort I made another terrible mistake. I went onto the internet.

Take any anti-depressant medication, type it into Google plus "side effects" and you will come up a with an unending catalogue of first-person tales of impossible distress, horror and ruined lives. As any doctor will tell you, the internet is not the best place to get your medical advice. On the other hand it does seem to be the perfect spot for people wishing to vent their dissatisfaction with the large pharmaceutical companies. I read it one evening, and only just had enough sense finally to turn it off after an hour or so. But it was too late. I didn't sleep at all that night and rang the doctor in a panic the next morning. The following night I didn't take the anti-depressant and managed to drift off to sleep easily. So logic dictated that this drug was keeping me awake, and not sleeping was the very thing which had made me so ill in the first place.

Into this fragile mix of pompous doctoring, internet diagnosis and sleep deprived semi-madness, I threw another wild card. I had been continuing to see my faith healer before and after my hospital admission. After a couple of sessions on my return home I started to feel that finally she was doing me some real good. She had a definite theory about my "coming through" to some sort of new spiritual dimension and how this marvellous outcome was imminent. I started to believe that the sleep and sedation was what had prompted this possibility. She was negative about medication, saying that anti-depressants were very upsetting to my body. I wanted to believe every word she said. As I started to feel better, I gave her the benefit of the doubt. I believed that the drugs would just keep me stuck, whereas her alternative was one of opportunity and progress but if I took the drugs, I would not get the benefits of this promised experience. So I went off the drugs and for a couple of weeks felt much better without the side effects. Before, naturally enough, starting to go rapidly downhill again.

It is important to understand the insanity of

someone who is not well mentally. It's not the same insanity of the 'mad' person who thinks that things which are not real are real, but it is instead the very unwise nature of the behaviour, of decision making, of negative choices evidenced by the mentally unwell patient which are so debilitating. This is a terrible problem with mental health treatment. If you break your leg, you go to the doctor. You then use your brain (not broken) to choose to take his or her advice on how to fix your leg (broken). Usually you just do what you are told. But when the problem is your brain, which is broken, unfortunately you are in rather less good a position to make and follow the sensible decisions regarding your treatment. Of course it would help if mental health treatment was as routinely successful as treatment for a broken leg. It isn't. Nowhere near. But, equally, mental health treatment, and the science around it, might be more effective if it wasn't for the brokenness of the brains we use to understand and manage it. I was obviously quite mad in this sense, but I was also having severe difficulty with the medication, which is not uncommon. What I needed was someone else – practically anyone who wasn't me – to be able to tell me carefully and with compassion and care what to do. Sadly, that wasn't included in the astronomical fees at the hospital, which seemed seriously to ration both time and kindness, so it left me no choice but to make up my own mind about my treatment, with a predictably poor outcome.

It was 2009 and getting on for the summer. Although I was beginning to feel worse, we had a long holiday to Greece – which is where my wife is from – in the offing. Like many people, I thought that perhaps all I needed was a good break in the sun. Certainly our usual retreat of a caravan near the sea in rural Greece was one of my favourite places and in August it was usually hot enough to stop even the most committed of neurotics from over-thinking too drastically. We were going for a month to the middle of nowhere. From the first day we arrived I knew that it was a mistake. Far from being relaxing, it was taxing. A new environment, a long way from home, with punishing weather, five children to care for and, most importantly, miles away from any kind of expert, practical or medical help for me. We ended up not having our usual holiday of frolics and adventures but were rooted on the beach, with a babe in arms. Taking up my own foetal position, I wasn't much more evolved than he was. Again I couldn't sleep. Waking up at three in the morning in your own bed is bad enough. Waking up in a boiling caravan is not an upgrade.

I had hoped to 'show up' for the kids a bit more on holiday. I did my best but I was frozen, just getting through the days, secretly counting the hours till I could get back to London and back to my spiritual healer, the only source of help I could imagine or hope for. Everything else appeared to be a dead end. Therapy, drugs, hospitals, doctors: all had failed to bring me anywhere close to the illusion of full remission from this living hell. My healer alone seemed to have it all planned out, as if she had no doubt at all about what was happening and what would be the end result. I would phone her from the beach when I couldn't bear it any more. She would support me, work on me from a distance, all unpaid. She was absolutely there for me, not exploiting me.

She was my only resource in a world which appeared to have abandoned me to an excruciating fate. I couldn't imagine coping without her. I had nothing left to lean on, but I was very seriously unwell. My wife nursed me the best she could, but with five young children to raise, her main contribution to my welfare was to make sure everything else was taken care of. The whole situation had put her under unimaginable strain and she was absolutely stoical in her response to keeping the family life going.

We had to move out of London because we couldn't afford to raise five children there and once we settled in our rural location, the future I was suddenly facing from this new perspective seemed irredeemably bleak. I was marooned in a small village, our house on a commuter run into town, and I would wake up on a Monday morning, early, terrified, anxious, and slowly watch the house come to life around me. Somehow, I would help with the school run, observe all the 'normal' people go to work in their cars, presumably from their houses, all paid for by their well-ordered lives. I, on the other hand, a lone figure of a man, would return home from the school run around 9am on a weekday and have nothing left to do but tremble. I would literally just stand in the hall, frozen, unmoving, unable to do anything useful at all. My wife carried on around me, sometimes furious, sometimes worried, sometimes caring, but mostly I think in denial. We both were. I didn't think of myself as mentally ill. People would say things like, "Well you lost your money but at least you have your health," and I would actually agree with them, wondering why thinking that didn't make me feel better. But I was in fact very much devoid of my health, and decided to have another go with the medical solution. My step-mother found a doctor through a referral from her own GP and eventually I went off to see him in his cosy practice in the Cotswolds. Another doctor; another fat fee; my same sorry tale of woe and desperation for immediate help; more promises of a miracle cure by way of medication.

So I tried a new anti-depressant. Within an hour or two of swallowing this new poison, I felt violently suicidal. Again, it just didn't agree with me. I had been terrified before taking it and held out for a week or so, but in the end I was just too desperate. This left me in the worst of all possible situations. By succumbing to the need to take it, I had acknowledged to myself that I was desperate but doing so had left me feeling even worse. I stopped the pills immediately and yet this alleviated nothing. The cosy Cotswolds doctor said something like, "Well, ok, so it ruined your day but didn't damage your brain!" and gave me another pill to try. I didn't. Yet.

In fact, I tried acupuncture instead. I had been given a recommendation by my supervisor who had become my therapist. This new option was also extortionate but, again, so was my need. Within moments of the acupuncturist's needles hitting my skin, I did feel a curious sense of relief. It seemed to release something and calmed me down. But the next morning I woke up early, as usual, in an even worse state than before. I went back again and was told that it could make me worse before I got better – as with medication, a familiar story. The problem was that I couldn't take being any worse than I already was. I had touched the bottom of hell. Or so I thought. But there was further yet to go.

I would go to London to see my spiritual healer regularly. It was my only relief from this nightmare merry-go-round of attempted treatments. Usually it bought me a few hours of feeling slightly less ghastly and also the promise – well, a verbal one at least – of recovery round the corner. I was addicted to both, but also running out of steam. I was becoming unrecognisable to myself and others. When I looked in the mirror I didn't know who I was looking at any more. I remember vividly the pale, tortured ghost looking back at me. I couldn't identify with him at all. A friend came to visit me for the weekend and later she told me that she left seriously frightened wondering what on earth I was doing not in hospital. I was starting definitively to despair and to give up. In one session with my spiritual healer, I was lying face up on her treatment table and she was waving her hands over me as usual. She often said that I needed to "let go", and on this particular occasion I felt as if I couldn't take it anymore. I had hit the wall with my capacity to bear any more mental anguish. I really didn't care what she did to me, just as long as something, anything changed. I can't remember if I said this or just thought it, but what came next is seared in my memory like a branding iron on the back of my brain.

I started to shake a little, which worried me, as always. She told me this was good and to continue to "let go". Trusting her, and no longer caring at all for my own welfare, I went with it. She held my feet and started shouting , "Get out, go". This was even weirder. I asked her what was going on and she said that there was an evil spirit which needed to leave me and I needed to let it. Part of me was highly alarmed by this world-view, but then again another part of me actually could see the logic. There was something desperately wrong with me; I was not myself; no-one could help me; perhaps this was a viable explanation which opened up the possibility of a way out? I continued to shake more and more, becoming increasingly anxious, but also strangely excited at the same time that something new was happening. Anything new had to be better than everything that had gone before, so spelt hope, surely? So I went with it. We continued with this surreal tussle for a while. She called the demon out and I carried on shaking, wondering what on earth was going on, but at that point giving myself up to any eventuality. Finally she said that she needed to take me downstairs to her husband, who was the real expert at this work. He was a fascinating character whom I rarely saw, but he seemed more than comfortable with the idea of his own particular gifts. He laid me down on a bed, sat next to my head and said in a calm commanding tone, "Come on, time to go out now."

Then I started to understand what was happening. Whereas before when I said I had been shaking, I had been probably trembling, now I began to flail around like a scarecrow caught in a tornado. I remember my arms and legs bouncing wildly on the bed and then my whole body starting to bounce up and down with it. I must have been screaming or crying out because my healer returned to the room and held my head. All the time they were saying things about someone coming out but were not telling me anything more than that. I began to freak out. If the body's capacity for anxiety is 100 points, I had walked through the healer's door that day at about 98. During this experience I think the figure went up to a seismic 1000. I was out of my mind in every possible way. I tried to stop it, sitting up, looking at them wildly but they told me to lie down and carry on. I obeyed. My limbs flung themselves around the bed more vigorously that it would have been possible to do on purpose. I was disconnected from my body; it was running its own show. And then, suddenly, in a fraction of a moment, it stopped. I went entirely [cut] limp all over and just slid off the bed. I ended up slumped on the floor looking up at them both. My healer said that it was finished now and that I should probably have a cup of tea and a biscuit. Then she went back upstairs to her waiting client.

I had to ask, of course, much as I was loathe to do so: was that an exorcism? "Oh, yes," came the quite matter of fact reply. Apparently he has to do it for his wife regularly; an occupational hazard for the spiritual healer. As bonkers as it sounds, I did actually feel better, somehow more myself. I was massively over agitated from the experience itself, but something, somewhere in me felt different. If it makes any sense at all, I did feel less 'possessed', more free and more me. Again, I connected with some hope! I had been attending a church after doing the Alpha course and there was quite a lot of talk of the supernatural there, of angels and demons, God and the Devil. So maybe they were all right. Maybe I had just been possessed, which explained why no-one had been able to help me. Perhaps going to church had brought me to the attention of the demons, who didn't like my new affiliation with Jesus. It all made sense; sort of. But I really did feel still very freaked out by this explosive experience. I presumed that my disquiet and over-excitation would just die down, but I presumed wrongly.

I returned home, picking up one of our children on the way. The mother of his friend asked politely about my day. I was tempted to say, "Not bad, trip to London, exorcism, just got back". I felt like a madman wondering around in a normal world. My sense of being more present in the world felt better, but the agitation was becoming worse. Over the next week or so, the promised miraculous recovery did not materialise somehow. I think my system had been pushed beyond a point it should ever have been made to go, and now it just did not have a way back. I had some pills like Valium. I hated taking them because they made me feel so groggy and drowsy so I would often wrestle with whether or not to take even half of one. Thoughts of killing myself persistently presented themselves but I managed instead to force the pills down me. They helped, a bit, but their effect would wear off reliably and then I realised that I was back where I started, or worse. I suppose this had happened before, but not in this way. Up until this point I had always been able to rely on the odd, if nebulous, glimpse of remission. Not this time. In some ways I was more 'myself', my brain a bit clearer, if barely perceptively. But my body was saturated more than ever with the symptoms of anxiety. Now all I could do almost all of the time was to hold onto myself and shake.

I was not recovering in any shape or form. I started into the final stage of severe, chronic suicidal thinking. The fantasies were now exclusively about allowing myself to die, about killing myself. Most people know what it is like to have a fleeting moment of wishing they weren't alive. Life is hard and at times anyone might suppose that death would seem a reasonable option, but the normal processes of self-preservation kick in more often than not, and the amazing thing is that human beings all over the place, in all kinds of circumstances so frequently find the inner resources to survive. We are good at it. So something is seriously wrong when the thinking about the desire for death persists, starts to take hold, and begins to become the cognitive norm.

It had been a thought for me since the summer. It was what drove me to ask for help and to be admitted to hospital in the first place, but then it was a kind of desperate, agonised cry for help: "I feel like I want to die, please help me not to do so." What I noticed in that hospital was that many of the patients there talked openly of their desire to kill themselves and how they might do it, comparing notes on whose insurance policy would be invalidated and how, by various causes of death, all of which was very dispiriting since many of them had been in there for several weeks. When I heard these stories in a group session, I could not identify with their sentiments. At that time, I had definitely wanted to live. I had just witnessed the birth of my fifth child. I wanted to get well, to provide for him and to be healthy, back in my family. I still had my survival instinct intact. This was beginning to disintegrate.

Gradually I would think about suicide more and more. It was like a dangerous game. When I thought about it or, more specifically, the being dead, rather than the actual killing myself, it brought me comfort.

It was a relief that I might actually be able to take some action to relieve my suffering; nothing else seemed to work and I was out of options. But then of course it was scary. I would come back to my awareness that I was having these thoughts, and from a different part of my brain this seemed deeply alarming, and not comforting at all. So I would flirt with this thinking, but not hang out with it much. I had been like that for a while, fairly stable in this somewhat benign stage of suicidal yearning. But with this new injection of crisis into my mind and body, somehow I ran out of steam. I started to go over to the dark side. I was being firmly seduced by the fantasy of death.

I remember very clearly waking up on a Saturday morning, very early as usual, in an agony of anxiety, desperate to sleep again, and going through my usual mental gymnastics of trying to find a way to relax. Pretty soon I was sketching out my detailed plans for my own death; and it was a blissful relief. There were a few options. It was hard to get the balance right between what would be bearable for me and too dreadful for the family. For example, my favourite fantasy was to bleed to death in a nice warm bath, which I thought would be relatively painless and tranquil, however I could see that this would be an awful scene for a family member to stumble upon. These ruminations did relax me, so I carried on. I thought about my insurance policy, who would find me where, how I would leave a note, what I would say. I had a bizarre idea about putting it on the internet, like a webpage, so that it would be easy to find and not get lost, but always struggled with how I could possibly explain all of this to my bereaved, fatherless children. In the way that we can all make plans in the dark hours before dawn, I got into a detailed, very real world in which this was something which I was going to be able to make happen. And then I snapped out of it. Another part of my brain kicked in, the part perhaps with some fight left in it and it gave me a new perspective on myself, observing rather than indulging in my thinking. I realised what I had been doing.

As a trained psychotherapist I am aware of the stages of suicidal thinking. Once you start making detailed plans, you are very close to putting that plan into action. I reviewed the flowchart from occasional despair to taking steps such as buying a rope and realised that I was one step away from my own death, and that this now well-trodden path was becoming all too familiar. Somehow it seemed like this was only going to go one way. I was devastated, terrified and horrified at the thought but that did not stop it coming thick and fast. The poison of suicidal fantasy had gained an irreversible hold on me. What was left of the rational part of me, which was observing this going on, was beginning to shrink and to whither. My desire to keep it alive was diminishing. I was beginning to let go, and no longer minding. I thought of my wife and what I thought was that she would be better off without me. I thought of my children. And that is where I hit a problem.

I had grown up with a dead parent and, clearly, the way things were turning out for me, that seemed to have been a poor start in life. Did I want to condemn my children to the same fate? I realised was that I did not. As far gone as I was, I could not give myself permission, not yet, to kill the father of my children.

Neither for myself, nor for my wife did I feel this level of resistance; only for this precious, innocent, lovely, adorable, vibrant, caring and talented pool of innate human potential. I so wanted to see them grow into the amazing people that they clearly could become. To cut them off from that at this very young age, inflicting on them a permanent, irreversible wound seemed to be the very antithesis of what it meant to be a father. Even wrestling with fringes of insane torment as I was at that moment, I was somehow still able to access the part of me that could not allow me to bestow upon them the same fate that the loss of my mother seemed to have had so disastrously bequeathed to me.

I found another gear and decided to take immediate action.

I called my step-mother at home in London and told her that I needed to go into hospital immediately or I would kill myself either today or tomorrow. Not an easy call to receive, I imagine. I think that her first response was probably typical, hoping that this was just a bad moment and that everything would be ok in a few hours. No, I was deadly serious. Having already been to the allegedly best hospital around, and knowing that that was the last thing I needed, I asked her to try to find the psychiatrist I had been seeing, the one I was referred to by her doctor, and to find out what hospital he would recommend. She did not seem that keen on me going to hospital but said that she would try to find the doctor. I would have to wait. I don't think that someone who has never felt like this can understand the awfulness of being asked to wait while feeling like this. Somehow that always my experience of psychiatry. I wouldn't call on it until I was absolutely desperate – and then I would always be asked to wait.

The answer eventually came about four hours later. She had spoken to the doctor and he recommended going to the local NHS crisis team. This was a blow. I knew enough about mental health by now to know that if the poshest hospital in London wasn't going to help me, then the local NHS (National Health Service) hospital was unlikely to be a great alternative. I had already been to the NHS GP (General Practitioner), who had referred me to the local counselling service and assured me I would get a letter in four to eight weeks (not treatment, just a letter). I told him I couldn't cope with four to eight minutes. My case had then graduated to secondary care in the NHS at a local mental health service. After a stressful and long wait of some weeks for an appointment and an assessment, I was told that I had untreated depression and was recommended for CBT therapy: the very thing which had proved so useless for me during my hapless sojourn in the private hospital. It was like being on a very slow merry-go-round. So my confidence in the NHS to save my life at this point was low. My life was at risk and to hear my step-mother telling me that she wasn't supportive of my going to any more private treatment felt like the end of the world.

I did have one wildcard. A friend of mine who was a therapist had been telling me for months to go to a large rehab and hospital facility in Arizona where she had once been a patient. She said that I was stuck in my 'trauma' and that they would know how to get me out of it. The problem was that she had been saying the same thing about almost everything and anybody for about a decade since she herself had been treated there. There had been moments when honestly I thought that if I had a paper-cut she would have told me to go there for treatment. In addition, I had the not insignificant problem that I could not leave my house without my wife. The thought of getting on a plane, let alone spending weeks in a clinic on my own, was beyond alarming. There was no way I could even consider it, so I had always discounted it as an option. Now I found myself on a Saturday afternoon in a museum, ostensibly with my children, but really just juggling phone calls from different government services, including one from social services asking me if I was going to kill children, or just myself. As I mooched around glass cabinets of priceless fascinating relics, I felt like the real museum was life itself, going on all around me. That was the lost experience I was visiting, cut off from it as if it was itself behind a thick wall of glass. I was watching people laughing, talking, looking at things, imagining that they were capable of having friends, of working, of taking care of their lives and those of others. I realised that I could no longer relate to their normal world at all, not even 1%. I was completely cut off and adrift from reality. I had basically reached the end. So, I left the museum, alone, and under a cloudless sky wandering adrift, untethered to my family, I found a signal for my mobile phone and called Arizona.

I was quoted a high price for a five-week stay. It was more money that we had in the whole world. I called my step-mother to discuss it. She hated the idea and said that it was too expensive. I remember leaving the museum and pacing the streets, thinking of the times she had said to me that "nothing is more important than your health" and knowing that my father could pay for this treatment a hundred times over and still have enough money left for the rest of his life. And I remember being completely ill-equipped to deal with the devastating, subjective implication that I made of this: that my life was proving too expensive to be worth saving. The shock of being kicked when already so far down was too much too process, so I found myself oddly detached and able to be pragmatic. There and then, I rang the hospital again and asked if they could help with the fees. Perhaps fifteen minutes later they called me back and offered me the treatment for a fraction less than all the money that we had in our bank account. For the first moment that day I saw a ray of hope. I could actually go if I needed to. We could not spare the money but we did actually have it in the literal sense. It would leave very little for my family, but it might save my life. And that seemed like the only viable option.

In the meantime I had booked to go to the local NHS crisis team, as recommended. I reported to reception of a local mental hospital and eventually a young psychiatrist and a nurse came to inspect me. We went into a small room and I told them my story all over again. I was due to see my private psychiatrist the following Tuesday, and it turned out that he had once run their team. I did say that I wasn't feeling quite so suicidal now that it was late in the afternoon. The young psychiatrist then said that he had seen me on television and was sure that I would make a full recovery. He didn't think that they should admit me to the hospital and thought that I could wait until my appointment a few days hence to see my psychiatrist. The hospital itself was predictably grim and I didn't much want to be admitted there either, but I was not in the least bit reassured by his prognosis. Just because he'd seen me on television didn't mean I wasn't dreadfully unwell. Also I failed to see how seeing my psychiatrist three days later would help. I needed the right kind of residential care immediately, or the consequences could be catastrophic. I felt very strongly that my life was at risk, but no-one seemed to want to know. I didn't tell my wife. I didn't want to worry her, because this was no cry for help. I actually didn't have much confidence that I would survive this and telling her that seemed cruel. I eventually crawled to bed at home with nothing decided or resolved, battered, broken, devastated by the indifference of both family and the medical services, hoping that my slight lift in mood would hold. Vain hope.

The next morning was identical to the previous one. I woke up early and began to become more resigned to my suicidal fantasies. Each time you go round this loop, there is a loss in resilience to resist it. I could feel my resolve slipping even further than before. I played the situation forward in my mind and knew that if I woke up like this again the next morning, a Monday, with all of the despair that that usually brought for me anyway, I would not survive the week. I went downstairs and booked the flight to Phoenix for that afternoon. Luckily it was late autumn so the flights were reasonably cheap. I then called the hospital and told them that I was coming in. Next I called my father and informed him. He thought it was mad, but I remember him saying something along the lines of at least I was making a decision. Somehow, though, his only significant comment was that it seemed that I was going there for the weather, it being a cold dreary November in England. Then I told my wife. I didn't tell her about the suicidal thinking, just that I was going away for five weeks to a high-end American treatment centre and that I would be using just about all of our money to do it. It cannot be said she exactly embraced the news. She was furious, and clearly devastated.

She drove me to the airport with our five children in the back. Everyone was very quiet. My wife wasn't speaking to me. When they left me at the airport terminal, my children's faces were ashen. The older ones looked terribly distressed, my middle child was screaming, the younger two more perplexed. I'll never forget the looks on their faces as I closed the door to walk away. I had no idea if I would live to return to see them again. I could detect their desperate sadness and panic that I was leaving. I knew the only way not to leave them forever was to leave them now, but equally I had no idea if what I was doing would work, or even if I could go through with it. Walking away was an agony on top of all my other agonies. My wife and children had been the only comfort in my life for nearly a year. I was now alone, misunderstood by my wife, wretchedly missed by my children, standing in the departures hall of Heathrow wondering where on earth I was going, in every sense, and why.

Once I made it to the departures lounge, I passed through that one-way door to this next phase of my treatment. I knew the only way forward was to get on that plane, but my resolve crumbled and with it the last vestiges of myself. All around me busy, happy people were getting on with their lives. I couldn't move. I stood still in one of the busiest thoroughfares in the world, frozen, immobile, undecided, unsupported. The world whisked by, hither and thither. I was like one of those people in a freeze-frame of a movie where all the other characters have been speeded up. I didn't belong there. No longer a member of this human race. I was hopelessly out of place and out of my depth. All I could do was cry. And that is what I did. As far as I could tell, nobody noticed; busy lives bustling by.

As I stood there with the airport terminal milling around me, gripping the railings of the skyway balcony, I only had one resource. I got out my phone and dialled the hospital in Arizona. The phone was answered by the nurses' station, it being the middle of the night there and, bless them, they took care of me. I don't know how they do it, but the nursing staff were angels. They talked me through getting going again and finding my way onto the plane. They assured me that once that door closed behind me, they had me from there on in. They would pick me up at the airport and get me well. They advised me to take some Valium and keep moving. Without that call I might have ended up going over that balcony, not moving on from it. That phone call was the departure point from which I stopped looking back – at the faces of my devastated children and distraught wife; from the life I had lost; from the world which I might never know again. And from which I started to look forward – to a place I'd never been; to people I'd never met; and to the promises of the healing which had proven so elusive. I walked away from my people, my country and my life and threw my future into the hands of something I knew almost nothing about. It was a total commitment. I was spending all of our money and if it didn't work for me I was at the very end of the road. I had to let go of the past and believe in a new beginning, a new treatment method and a new outcome.

I surrendered myself, utterly, on every level, to that aeroplane. The airline thankfully did the rest.

I was on my way.

4 RECOVERY

I entered the American treatment centre in Arizona and so began the hardest five weeks of my life. I was very, very ill. The plane trip over had been torture. I had tried to cope with the long flight by watching films. I hadn't been able to watch television for a long time by then because everything would seem to trigger an overwhelming reaction in me. Anything traumatic, violent or harmful would be too much, making me feel like my body was spiralling out of control with physical anxiety but, equally, anything wholesome, happy or loving was too painful too. I couldn't bear to see people's homes, their pain, their happiness, their health and their dramas. Everything, literally everything, triggered an adverse reaction in me and was too much to bear. Now I was thousands of miles away from home surrounded by strangers. I was out of control, out of my mind and out of my comfort zone.

The therapeutic programme at the hospital turned out to be a complete nightmare. Possibly I was just not well enough to be there in the first place. I was told after I'd been there for about three weeks that they had considered sending me away to a psychiatric hospital. Given that it was itself a psychiatric hospital, or so it said on its web-site, I assumed this meant something pretty serious. The psychiatrist who treated me there later told me that I was the worst case of anxiety she had seen during a twenty year career in both private and public mental health. She said being in the room with me was unbearable and she had to make jokes at my expense about my being British just to cope. My therapists were underwhelmed by me. They seemed to think that I was somehow creating my own problem and I don't think they much liked my lack of positive response to their methods. We were treated in groups and I couldn't get much out of this or contribute in any meaningful way. I needed processing, not information, but unfortunately the main treatment at this hospital was a cognitive programme for supporting recovering addicts. It didn't fit my needs, but at least I was safe. Or so I thought.

I really struggled in the company of the large number of other patients there because it was so hard for me even to speak. Sometimes I would sit at the big round tables in the cafeteria and, though I would want to make friends, to laugh and joke with the others, I really couldn't. I often couldn't actually speak at all. I realised that I had lost all capacity to connect with my personality, to show people who I really was. My anxiety was so bad that most of the time I could only shuffle around. I focused on little other than trying to understand what was on my schedule for the next fifteen minutes and keeping busy. There wasn't much to do outside of this programme, so most people passed their time when not in therapy just talking to each other. I couldn't do this, so I found myself wandering from one thing to another, pointlessly creating tasks for myself, just for the sake of it. I would go and check for messages in the nurses' section, or look at my schedule, browse the bookshop, go to a meeting not relevant to me. The good thing was that I was busy and, even better than that, I showed up for absolutely everything just to have something to do.

The first week passed in a disorientating daze. My wife was both furious and concerned about me. I spoke to her briefly every morning. I couldn't bear to think about my children and wanted every day to leave and go home to them. I had to hang on to the idea that I would be able to do that in five weeks. The therapy group was painful to me. We were just learning mainly about addictions and every time I had to do anything, like for example a 'first step' exercise on depression (as if it was some sort of addiction); I couldn't do much more than just weep. I remember I spent the whole of one morning's group session just crying about my life. The therapist tried to convince me that I had some kind of adult 'on board' by which she meant that I could substitute my collapsed child-like state for that of a capable adult at will. It was valiant work, but misplaced and could not help me in that condition. I had more luck with the psychiatrist.

Although she teased me about it, she could actually accept that I was very sensitive to my medication. She started me on a very low dose of a new anti-depressant and, to her credit, did not baulk at attempting to answer my incessant questions about the dose, the precise time to take it, the tiny adjustments to be made, and nor did she appear to resist navigating my hyper-vigilant anxiety. She went with me on these things and spent fifteen or twenty minutes each day for that first week or so just counselling me onto this tiny dose of medication. The amazing thing was that it worked. For the first time since I had entered the medical process I was able to tolerate a drug for a week without any really appalling side-effects. She had to sedate me to sleep so I was constantly groggy, and the drug itself agitated me, but overall it was just about bearable. This was an unbelievably important step forward. It was supposed to take about four to five weeks to become effective. So I told myself that I simply had to stay there, cope with the programme minute by minute, and then I would be able to return to my family in five weeks for Christmas, by which time I would no longer need to kill myself. Finally I had a plan, even if the execution of it was torture.

The only part of the actual programme which worked for me at that time was yoga. I had no idea at the time why and wouldn't for a long time get a glimpse into the truth of what was actually wrong with me which would explain it. The teacher would bring recordings of spiritual teachings and after a mild yoga session we would listen to these. The combination of body work and tranquillity would bring about the processing in my system that I seemed to be missing. I often ended the sessions sobbing deeply and would have moments of lucid recovery, too lucid probably, when I would glimpse what it might be like to feel well again. Then I would be back into the general programme again, which was very cognitive and behavioural. This makes perfect sense for a treatment centre which originated as an alcohol rehabilitation centre. It was not such a great idea for me.

The second week we went into a course run on the campus in small groups, in which outside participants also took part. I was the only inpatient in my group. It was quite shocking to see the difference between myself and normal functioning people. The workshop itself concentrated on gestalt work, a kind of therapy where the patient would hold a dialogue with someone in an empty chair. I remember starting the week so stressed about the course that I nearly couldn't go through with it, but equally I felt that it might possibly offer me some time to process things therapeutically and I couldn't bear to go back into more group behavioural therapy.

I finally got my turn to do the work on day four and an extraordinary thing happened. I spent an hour and a half crying, shouting, yelling and fighting with pillows, blankets and chairs. And, at the end of it all I miraculously felt completely free of stress and symptoms. I had entered that session with my body crumpled up in pain, my mind racing through its usual catastrophe of thoughts and my spirit crushed. And I emerged from it feeling something close to normal. It's really quite impossible to overstate how odd this was. When I say normal, I mean relaxed, calm, myself again, untroubled. I had not felt like this in over a year. I had been told that I might be able to feel like myself again if I took harmful medication for a few weeks. No one had mentioned to me that unburdening myself to an empty chair could do likewise. I went from absolute crisis to no symptoms at all in ninety minutes. This was surely impossible.

I thought of my spiritual healer and her insistence that I could somehow just let go and "come through to the other side". Was this what she meant? I thought of my friend and her dogged advocacy of this hospital and its miracle cure for trauma. Had she been right all along? I dared to believe that I was better now, that I wouldn't have to take the drugs anymore, that I could go home early, fully recovered.

Would I feel like this forever? I just had no idea. I went to the cafeteria for a break and was actually able to talk to some people. For the first time, I could take an interest in them and their problems, and was able to offer my typically calm reflections on what they were going through. They could get a sense of who I was for the first time and I had an opportunity actually to make myself likable and to connect with people. There was hope. I might even manage to enjoy myself and have some fun. It really seemed too good to be true.

Unfortunately, of course, it was. Serious psychiatric symptoms don't disappear just like that, in a pantomime flash. Something else must have been going on, but it was baffling, impossible to explain. Certainly the therapists seemed only able to guess at what had taken place. And just as I had ridden a powerful wave of recovery, so I sunk into the dreadful dip of relapse. I started to feel anxious again at the next session of our course. I hugged a pillow to my stomach to protect me from what I was watching as the next punter went through the empty chair routine. By dinner I realised that my brain was going through the same old loops. The morning was the same agony of desperation and futile attempts to sleep again. What the hell had happened to me?

The following week I asked to be transferred to a different group. Lovely as she was, my original therapist wasn't getting me anywhere and, if I'd learned anything from the previous week, it was that I needed process, not education. The only group available was the one to which the sex addicts were assigned and the therapist leading it was both their longest standing and, by reputation, the most brutal. Frankly I welcomed this. I had limited time and money to be there and didn't want to waste either of them. If she was willing to take me on and to not flinch from what must be my very serious needs, then I was happy to go there. I'm not sure if this was the best or worst thing that happened to me in treatment. It became in itself a whole new layer of torture, which was good because it distracted me from the hell I was otherwise in, but bad because it actually nearly did me in for good.

At the very end of the earlier 'trauma reduction course' session, I had been asked to put my dead mother in the empty chair and that seemed to make me stumble into some new territory. It had never occurred to me previously to consider how she must have felt when she was dying. She was a young woman of twenty-four, from an emotionally illiterate family which was typical of that time and place, and she had a new baby. Clearly it was going to be difficult. I knew from her best friend that my mother had probably been in denial (she never wrote a will), as had, I assume, her whole family. There was a doctor in Boston who suggested that he might cure her and so I suppose that was their hope. The whole point of this course I was on was to identify the emotions which caregivers had been unable to bear, and therefore which we, as children, would have taken on or internalised for them. Suddenly I was seeing how the anxiety and fear which had been such a huge backdrop to my adult life might actually be a residue from the unprocessed emotions which my mother had been unable to bear for herself. This realisation came over me in a somatic way at the end of this session. It was an experience, not a thought, but there was no time to go anywhere with it. However, the genie was out of the bottle and once these things have begun, there is no going back.

The following week, just as I changed groups and therapists, I started to feel completely overwhelmed again, but rather differently than before. Previously I had been plagued simply by extreme symptoms. My anxiety had my body in a rictus, I could hardly talk, I would shake, not sleep and so forth. I was miserable, depressed, scared and worried, but these were all relatively normal reactions to the state I was in and how my life was going. Now something new started. I couldn't identify it or really name it. It was as if the volume and volatility on my internal world had been turned up dramatically, like taking a frozen lake of gas, deep in the basement of a dormant volcano and starting to melt it into steam. Once started, there seemed to be a chain reaction, accelerating this meltdown alarmingly. My system was starting to give vent to itself, but the pressure that it began to exert on me was threatening to rip me apart.

The type of treatment I was in was clearly not the right one for me at the time, valuable as it was proving for many of my fellow inmates. How was I supposed to process the kinds of feelings I was having in a treatment group session in which I was listening to someone do an 'inventory' of his crimes of sexual acting out with young women, or watching as his denial about what was and wasn't ok was stripped bare by our uncompromising therapist. This was no help to me at all. I needed something completely different but I wasn't finding it. I was wobbling around the campus like an unexploded bomb, and the fuse was lit.

I went to my new therapist and asked for help at the end of our group. She told me that I had survived for forty years so she was sure I would be all right until the morning and asked me to see her after breakfast. I clung on. I put all my will power into surviving the evening, the night and the dawn. I watched the clock and turned up at her door at the appointed time. She answered and looked surprised to see me, irritated even. She said that she was having supervision in her office with some other therapists and I would have to come back later for the group session. I was devastated. I desperately needed help. I had been propelled into this new state during the workshop the previous week and now, even though I was apparently paying for the highest possible level of 24-hour care, there was no-one to pick up the pieces of what this hospital had done to me and to help me. The sense of abandonment was unbearable. My current situation seemed to be a replica of the problem of the past which I had come to America precisely to try to overcome. Barely able to walk, I stumbled down to the nurses' station and asked the astonishingly patient staff there if they would help me. Of course they did. One of them took me into a small consulting room and I just fell apart.

I cried so hard and for so long that I thought I would do myself an internal injury. I was completely saturated with the experience of being totally bereft. My entire soul seemed to shake with terror, loss and sadness. I was so wracked with grief that I actually fell off the chair and onto the floor. Even in this state I was aware enough to follow the 'no touching without permission' rule and asked the nurse if she would hold my hands. She kindly did so, but clearly had absolutely no idea how to deal with me. After about fifteen to twenty minutes of this I think she got worried enough to call for back up. The head of the counselling team was wheeled in to see me. I was slightly recovering but still unmanageably distressed. I had never seen him before and assumed that he must be their top therapist, but my world rather dissolved around me when he started treating me with the same CBT method that had been employed at the Priory and from which I had scarpered. He asked me what the thought was that I had had just before I became so distressed. I understand that if I think to myself, "I'm never going to get another job," I will distress myself, obviously, but this had been on a totally different scale. There had not been any thought, just a torrent of non-verbal, probably pre-verbal, distress. The idea that I could have done this to myself with some lazy thinking was ludicrous. I was totally shocked to realise that I was back in a therapeutic black hole, more aware of what I needed than were the people I was paying to treat me, and yet still a million miles away from being able to fix myself, or knowing who could do it for me.

Gradually I recovered over the next hour or so and they all went back to work. I had to go to a group session and somehow stumbled through the morning, but I could feel the same emotional tsunami building up again. It did not help that my group now included people who were there for their own rather strikingly difficult reasons, such as being on the way to jail for such things as stalking and photographing underage girls. Not quite the ideal environment for me, at that moment.

By lunch time I was melting down again. I went back to the nurses' station and asked if I could sit in one of their rooms. I waited there and again fell apart, sobbing uncontrollably, slumped on the floor hugging a chair to try to keep upright. But this time nobody came. I thought this was odd, but they were often busy there with the high need patients like me. I managed to process some of my emotional overload on my own and felt somewhat better for it. That afternoon I had to sit in on another group member's family session, which was our typical afternoon schedule. At least that would take the focus off me for a while. Things surely could not get any worse than our hard-core morning groups and it gave me a chance just to try to calm down. At some point during this session I began to feel a slight positive tug at my system, perhaps a dividend of the exhausting emotional overload of the morning. I thought maybe I might be starting to turn the corner. But my excitement was short lived.

At the end of the group I was asked to stay behind. The scary therapist was joined by her intern and the family therapist, a veteran of the treatment centre. Suddenly the mood in the room seemed quite different, like visiting the headmaster. I was able, briefly, to assert that I had had a terrible day but was beginning to feel a bit better, when I was assaulted by what I can only reflect upon in retrospect as a therapeutic intervention of utter madness. I was faced by the three of them with stern body language and expressions, and then this rather business-like young lady bluntly accused me of being a histrionic baby, castigated me for my "performance" in the nurses' station, admonished me for touching the nurse and holding onto her and I was then told to grow up. They told me that the nurses had now been instructed not to help me anymore and that if I was to behave like this again I would be transferred out to a maximum security psychiatric hospital where I would be left on my own in a bed. I was also put on a 'no touch' and 'no female contact' contract, which meant that I couldn't talk to any woman or touch anyone at all. This was written on my name tag which I wore around my neck. Some of my best friends in there by now were women, there being more of them in treatment than men. All of them were now off limits. Finally, I was told to go and buy a book called, "Growing Myself Up" and invited to follow the instructions. I was totally flabbergasted.

My moment of feeling an inkling of recovery was blown to smithereens. I was assaulted by new anxieties in every direction. In a few minutes they had ripped away from me most of my friends and many of my other sources of security and comfort in recovery. Everything I had come to rely on to get through these few weeks was demolished. I had had to believe in these people, to trust that they knew something new which could get me well. This was obliterated. Their own treatment protocol had made me so unstable and now they were blaming me for being upset! I just couldn't believe it. Obviously, though, they weren't reacting to nothing. I was incredibly irritatingly babyish in many ways, or 'wounded' as they would have said. My whole demeanour was that of the beleaguered infant who was drowning in abuse and too small to fight back. I was needy, and desperate and probably very annoying. I was weak and lame; perhaps unhelpful at times or uncooperative simply because I was so stressed and so unhappy, difficult to be around because I was so miserable; and, I'm sure, irritatingly unsatisfying to treat, because I was not getting any better. Nothing they were doing was helping much, and they were used to scoring much better results than I was providing.

But I was also very ill. The problem with this treatment programme was that it was exclusively behavioural and therefore they took the view that they should reboot my behaviour without looking first at what might have been making me so unwell. There is a time and a place for both in treatment and unfortunately, in this case, their judgement was wrong. How wrong, I wasn't to learn for many weeks, but in the meantime, I was left to pick up the pieces alone.

I clearly wouldn't have admitted myself to hospital if there I hadn't been desperately in need. The only people who seemed willing to help me were in the nurses' station and were now not allowed to. And I had been told that if I showed any more distress over this I would be ejected from the facility, to a fate I could not imagine or probably afford, either financially or mentally. To cap it all off, I was no longer allowed to talk to half the people I knew and anyone who did not already know me, now assumed from the information on my badge that I was a sex addicted threat to all womankind. In my lowest moment of emotional disturbance, they had cut me adrift from everything I believed would help me and everyone who was supporting me. I was even more anxious and distressed than when I had arrived at the campus on my first night.

I wandered around outside in a daze for hours. There were places you could find at the back of the campus where no one really went. I walked there, round and round, trying to gather myself, my thoughts, my sense of self. I just didn't know what to do. This scary therapist who had known me for all of two days, and then only through seeing me in groups, had just kicked down the door to my psychic world and trampled all over it with hobnail boots. She clearly was not a good fit for my needs. On the other hand, the psychiatrist was helping me. I was two and a half weeks in and had so far been able to tolerate the medication. Surely things would improve in a week or two. I had nowhere else to go. I would not be safe at home. I had no strength to make any choices or to travel anywhere. I was unravelling anyway and had no chance of taking care of myself outside of a residential setting. I was trapped, stuck, in a place where the one person who should have been helping me was attacking me. My anxiety went through the roof. I could feel myself beginning to combust again, but I wasn't allowed to. I couldn't hold this in much longer, but was terrified of being shipped out to a psychiatric hospital. I went to the nurses' station and asked for something to calm me down. They gave me a benzodiazepine. I then took myself off to the back of the lot, hid and cried.

I had spent my family's last penny and had left my wife and young children to come all the way across the world on the promise and hope of a therapeutic solution to my problems and a treatment for my 'trauma'. I was now drugging myself to numb these same emotions I came there to process, because they had been deemed unacceptable by an alleged therapeutic process. I was scared, hidden, alone with my torment, sobbing in pain but not allowed to reach out for any help from the staff. Surely this was a huge fucking mistake.

I staggered numbly to one of the treatment blocks which was on two levels and a slight incline. I made my way to the balcony at the back on the second level where the hill sloped away. No one was there and no one could see me. I looked down. It was high enough that if I threw myself off head first I could guarantee to break my neck. I thought about the freedom that this would bring and the punishment that it would deal out to all those who had failed me. I was of course furious with this therapist, but also all of the doctors back in the UK. My family too, my wife, my friends even. My father and step-mother had not supported me in coming for treatment. I became so distressed about this in my first week that I had to ask someone in the office if they would call him to ask if he would contribute to the cost. Leaving my wife with just enough for four weeks' groceries in the bank and no foreseeable means of future income was itself a huge trigger for my anxiety. I had asked my father by email when I left to try to help. No money had been forthcoming and the hospital asked me to pay. Before I did so I made them call him. I was so unwell that I couldn't bear to do it myself, fearing a total meltdown if he said no. In the end that was the result anyway. When I heard the news, I was so upset that I could not speak or eat for two days. I was at a loss to believe that my own father, a man worth many millions, could leave my family and me with nothing while I went to hospital to try to save my sanity, possibly even my life.

I had had no communication at all from any of my friends or family. Not an email, not a card, not a letter. The nurses' station was a busy conduit of such messages and presents for all the other patients. Every day there would be notices on the board of letters and packages to collect, little telephone message slips in a rotating stand on the desk; signs of care, connection and life outside treatment for everyone to cling onto. I never got a single message in my entire time in treatment. The nurses were so upset for me, seeing me checking the message box every day, twice a day, that they began to leave me their own messages, things like, "You are a valuable person"; "Keep going, you're going to be ok"; "You are perfectly imperfect". From my father, step-mother, half-brother, half-sister, the people I had grown up with, simulating a nuclear family, I heard nothing. From my wife and children, nothing, although I did call her every day. From my friends, again nothing. In all my time there I got one piece of mail, from a patient who had just left and wanted to say hi.

Looking back on it I realise that all these people weren't crazy. I had spent a lifetime being a selfish jerk. I withdrew from my friends when I got married because I needed my wife so much. I also never really felt quite right but couldn't admit it even to myself, let alone to friends whom I wanted to regard me still as capable and successful. I spent a lot of my time just hiding, either at home or in Greece. I dressed it up as a lifestyle choice, but really just couldn't do anything else. So gradually I just found myself less and less in relationship with the people I'd grown up with, my friends from school, university and life. This was a terrible loss, but one which I replaced with the comfort of my wife and growing family. I didn't have any space to think about it from my friends' point of view. On any given day, week, month, year, it just felt to me as if I was surviving. I would return to them later, return to myself later, one day, somehow, maybe. But that day never came and so I ended up more and more out on a limb with no one to lean on but my wife. I manipulated her to be more how I needed her to be because I could cope with so little, and no one else.

I used and abused family, in the same way, by relating to them when I needed them to help me to cope with something, only offering little or nothing in return. It felt to me at least as if this was not out of choice, but out of necessity. I never presented it as such though. I wanted to remain the hero, the successful oldest son. So as my life and myself became more and more out of control, their experience of me was just as someone there to gain from them what I needed to sustain my family. I thought I had no other way to do it. I gave very little back, only occasionally able to peer through the veil of my self-interest, and now I was reaping the dubious rewards of decades of ego-centric behaviour. In some ways I must have appeared to have been nothing but a rampant narcissist, manipulative, greedy, controlling, but I think that this was largely because of the illusion of the armour of my upbringing. Fairly close under the surface was an ocean of self-doubt, fear and panic. This wasn't what I was brought up to present to the world, though, so instead of being real with people and forging genuine relationships, I hid away and hoped I could do something to make them like me anyway.

I failed. And, at this point in the treatment and from my 'wounded' perspective, I was still unable to see my own part in this and so all I knew was the dreadful isolation, the heart-breaking realisation that, even when compared with a bunch of patients in a lunatic asylum, I was totally unique in being utterly adrift.

This was all in my mind as I stood on that balcony; I was alone, no-one would really miss me, no-one wanted me to get well and the people I was paying to do it for me were crazy. Suddenly those fifteen feet of air between me and the hard, rocky ground looked very tempting. I knew there was a way out, somewhere I could finally go to rest.

But my children.

I had made a deal with myself to live for five weeks to give the medication a chance, a chance for my children to grow up with a father who was at least alive, however inadequate he may be. I had made that bargain and I may have many flaws, but keeping my promises is not usually one of them. I absorbed the possibility of an easy, quick death but decided to put it on hold for the moment. On balance the pleasure of punishing everyone who had let me down didn't weigh up against the agony of deserting my children,

but at least I had the option. I had adapted. I still had
a plan, even if I had had to replace the therapy with a
balcony in order to believe that I could get some relief
from the awful hell in which I was immersed. I
decided to shelve my back-up plan for the time being.
I reckoned I could do another three weeks, and
acquired some more benzodiazepines. So it was I dug
in for the very worst therapeutic experience of my
life.

Group was hell: a constant diet of sex addiction
counselling and more assaults on my inability to
"grow up" out of what I assumed was a serious
medical condition. This was good work, done very
well, for the right patients, and many in my group
were eternally grateful to be there, but there were
some obvious flaws too when holding this up as
treatment for a mental illness. The intern one day
communicated to me her disappointment and anger
that the previous afternoon I had looked a little better
but then this morning I was very anxious again. She
was actually angry with me. Such was my vulnerability
that I didn't even point out to her that even the most
basic knowledge of anxiety and depression holds that
it is worse in the morning than in the afternoon. This
was bad enough, but I also noticed that I was finding
it strangely difficult to cope with what I was hearing
all around me. At least two of the members of my
group were there because their sex addiction bordered
on the criminal, or had actually been criminal, due to
their fascination with younger women, teenagers. I
have great respect for them for asking for help and
getting treatment, and for being willing to share this
very difficult material with a group, but what I
noticed was that I found it incredibly difficult to listen

to. I wasn't judging it, or judging them, just reacting in a very profound and uncomfortable way.

This difficulty went beyond what might be a normal aversion to hearing about unpalatable thoughts, actions and feelings. I noticed that I would get a feeling, like a kind of electricity in my gut, which would seem to me to be an exaggeration of all of my worst symptoms and that it would take ages, days sometimes, to ease. I tried to make sense of this. When I was twelve, at a prep school, the deputy head-master had taken a weird interest in me. He would offer boys sweets in return for being able to mock-beat them with a butter pat he kept in his briefcase. With me he seemed to be trying to take this game even further. He did actually beat me once, allegedly for discipline reasons, and would act out some rather creepy games with me too, like pretending to beat me with his slippers in the morning in his bedroom. He also once asked me to come to his study for a drink if I couldn't sleep. This was all in my last term at the school and looking back on it I realise that I just froze. It did not occur to me to tell anyone about this. Every time it happened, I just hoped that was the end of it and tried to forget about it. I just hung in there and hoped that it would go away, which looking back on it seems kind of odd. But as an adult, particularly in therapy, I have always been very angry about this and noticed that, especially when I read something about paedophiles, particularly in schools or churches, that I become very agitated. This, I speculated, was what was being stirred up in this group. I tried to broach it with the therapist but was, as usual, dismissed and told to grow up. It seemed that this was simply taken as yet another way for me to act as if it was OK to feel sorry for myself, and their whole strategy for me was to help me to find a different way to 'be'. However it skirted over a serious issue, one which I was only going to come to understand the depth of much, much later, and when I did, I looked back on these therapeutic experiences with horror.

Worse, though, my roommate was in my group and so it was I found out that he was having treatment before going to prison for downloading pictures of teenage girls onto his computer. He was being sent down for three years, so I always wondered if I had the whole story but, nonetheless, what I noticed was that I found it hard to sleep easily when he was around. This was a troublesome thing to observe, since I found it hard to sleep at all! But it did slowly dawn on me that once he got up in the morning and left the room I could get more rest and sometimes now even a little sleep. Again I brought this up in therapy, given my history with my housemaster at school, who literally slept down the hall from me every night, but was again shot down. I was told sharing a room with this man or continuing this group therapy, or both, would be good for me, a gift even. But in my body I had a different experience.

The agony of anxiety was stimulated anew and often shot through the roof in these groups, twice a day. The good news was that it gave me a real problem to deal with in the here and now, which in a funny way was better than feeling like that but with nothing obvious to be afraid of. It was, though, itself becoming a dreadful source of stress and that clearly was not to my benefit. Who is to say though, in retrospect, that it wasn't a blessing in disguise? I'm not all knowing, so I can't be sure if I should be grateful to that therapist or have a genuine axe to grind about the lack of understanding of my condition. She was brilliant with others, at the work she did best, but was just the wrong person for me. In the end it didn't matter. These weeks were going to be hell either way and at least I learnt about something new, and met some extraordinarily brave people on a deeper level than I would have done in the canteen. And, crucially, I started to notice something disturbing, dark and hidden about myself in relation to their stories of sexual addiction and the inevitable childhood abuse that prompted it, something which began a restlessness within me and which was going to take a long time to settle.

It wasn't all bad during those final three weeks in treatment. I discovered that there were weekend and evening counsellors available whom I could sign up to see. This was, I think, supposed to be a kind of overflow, emergency system. But I made it my routine. I would go every day, at least once, and turned this into my therapy. I went to recover from group. The counsellors were a fantastic rod of support. They were willing just to be there in the room with my hellish anxiety, and to listen. They held on to me psychologically and didn't judge me. The nurses, who were unstinting in their loyalty and support, quickly reverted to being there for me, and remained a spectacular source of comfort. I could take a wild guess that they were less well paid than any of the counsellors, and yet the time and effort that they would put in seemed to exceed anything else on offer across the campus. They brought a genuine care and compassion to their service which was always in excess of what they might have had to do.

Frankly, I don't know how they could have borne us. We were a hugely difficult, crazy, disturbed and upset bunch of deteriorated lunatics, but they would meet all of that madness with an easy charm and firm confidence in our recovery. Even so, it was the other patients who really kept me going.

In the midst of all of their own pain, loss and drama, they were the most compassionate and knowledgeable resource on the campus. Deep in their own processes, they were in touch with the really messy stuff of being human, such as our darkest thoughts, our most shameful desires and our most regretted deeds, which we all glide over in our normal everyday lives, and in doing so they became truly human. These were people would stop doing that thing we all do so easily, telling others what to do and how to live or feel, and instead replace it with the awful experience of being completely saturated in their own internal pain. In that place it was ok with them for me to be in pain too, and that was what made it a different experience, one that was truly safe. This lack of judgement borne out of giving up a lifetime of avoidance gave us the solidarity of a true brotherhood, something most of us, in our myriad of dysfunctions, had spoiled for ourselves in the real world a long time ago. It was a community of equals, with men and women of wildly diverse backgrounds, wealth and status. We always, always looked out for each other and that more than anything, at a time when no-one else on the planet seemed to be taking any interest in me, was worth the daily fee. Together we forged the tiny flicker of a flame of recovery; fragile, nervous, weak and tremulous, but burning nonetheless.

In my last week, after a slight increase in my medication, I started to sleep again in the mornings. This was a breakthrough moment. I had committed myself to five weeks in hospital to see if I could finally become stable enough on some medication not to want to kill myself and, four and a half weeks in, I appeared to be getting somewhere. If I could sleep, then everything would be different. I was still all over the place, but to be able to wake up slightly later in the morning and to experience some rest, almost exactly a year after I had stopped being able to sleep, felt like something to live for. It was possible that I had saved myself from an even worse state, but then the reality of dealing with my life came into focus. I was still a total mess and my world was shattered. I had no money or job, could not even contemplate the thought of working in mental health again, given how I was feeling, and therefore had no career. What I did have was a wife and five children depending on me to provide for them. It was untenable.

In one of my last groups, the therapist took me aside for a moment at the end and discussed with me my 'after-care'. I didn't even know what this was. She gave me three recommendations and made me sign a form saying that I had received them. They were for a much longer stay of therapy at some other clinics, including one on their own campus, a small specialist unit for longer-term trauma treatment. She did not tell me anything about them, or recommend one over the other, just ticked the box and let me get on with it. As part of my strategy of coping, I would always try to keep busy, so this gave me something new to find out about. I went to the business office and asked them a few questions about this trauma clinic.

They didn't seem to know much, for example what the daily routine might have been, what went on there, how exactly people were treated. They did have a very glossy brochure which advertised this treatment for "trauma", but after my experience on their trauma-busting course during my second week there, I was naturally rather suspicious of this. I did not have any money anyway and I was needed and due back home for Christmas, but I did keep asking questions.

I am not sure why I persisted down this line of enquiry – perhaps something to do, perhaps a sense that I needed to keep looking for help. I did manage to obtain a copy of the weekly schedule, which I was disappointed to see was rather sparse. When handing it to me the administrator happened to mention, almost as an afterthought, that the Clinical Director of the trauma clinic was in the patients' lounge every Tuesday lunch-time so I could ask her these questions myself. This wasn't advertised anywhere and I could easily have not known about it. In any case, I went along on my final Tuesday there and no-one was around, so I assumed she wouldn't be coming and trudged off to try to find something else to do. Failing, I made one of my despairing circuits back to the nurses' station to see if there had been any mail for me – no, of course not – and on my way I went past the window to the patients' lounge. I glimpsed my good friend in there with his wife at a table with another woman. Bored and curious I went in, to see what they were up to.

I could have missed it, taken another path, glanced a different way, asked a different question, passed by that window onto some more familiar chore. But I found my way into that room that day. And when I walked through that door to the patients' lounge, I opened the door for myself into a different world, a new life and a treatment where clinicians knew what was wrong with me, knew how to fix it and could help me to get well again.

I sat down at the table with my friend and listened to his conversation with Clinical Director, who ran the trauma centre. She seemed somewhat unremarkable, quiet even, and perhaps a little out of place in this rather manic place. Probably it was a bit of an anti-climax, but I was there really by default, just another stop along my way of deflecting my boredom and distress. She was talking to him about something to do with his nervous system and I wasn't paying much attention. Then she turned to me. She asked me what my problem was and I told her about my anxiety. As casual you like, she then just said, "Yes, I can feel it in my stomach. It's about here isn't it?" And she held her stomach exactly where I had been feeling totally stuck and desperate ever since the trauma course in my second week of treatment. I was astonished. She then asked the others to feel it too, and they could. We sat there for a moment, all feeling my 'body', whatever that meant!

It was extraordinary. I had spent four and a half weeks being told to grow up and now someone was finally validating what I had been trying to say all along: that there was something actually wrong with me that needed to be fixed. This quietly spoken, mild-mannered, trauma therapist knew what was wrong and said she knew what to do about it. And instantly I absolutely believed her. Within two minutes of meeting her it became entirely apparent that my search for accurate, successful treatment was over. I asked her what I could hope to get out of this clinic and she promised me my life back. She said I would get so well that I could go back to working in mental health, something which I had considered to be an absolute impossibility. I was still in a terrible state and the thought of hearing about another person's problems was just inconceivable, ever. It was another professional with yet another promise, but this time I believed in it because somehow she just embodied the knowledge that this was right and would work for me. I didn't have a moment's doubt. She told me that I needed at least four weeks there. And then I heard the price: another $10,000 at least. I did not have four weeks. I did not have four hours. What I did have was a wife and five children expecting me home for Christmas and an empty bank account.

Cheerfully I rang my wife and gave her the good news that I needed to stay out in Arizona for another month or so, and that she would have to find some money from somewhere, but I might actually become well enough again to work as a result. The response was not positive: there was no way I wasn't coming home and there was absolutely no money left.

I had spent all of my time, effort and money to reach the point of finding what I needed. Now that I was there, on the very brink of salvation after the longest year of my life and just as I had glimpsed the possibility of a real cure for whatever was wrong with me, with the invitation to renew my life and to begin again, I had nothing left – no goodwill, no money, no time; nothing other than a family who wanted me to come home, desperate for a husband and a father. Just when it seemed that I might rise again from the ashes of my life, the rubble of this bonfire seemed too great and it seemed like it would finally crush me.

I thought of the money that I had spent in my lifetime, on holidays, business deals, houses, fripperies and most recently, my treatment. Mere crumbs from that bloated cake of good living would save me now, a tax rebate, an unpaid lawyer's bill, a holiday not taken, but there was nothing. My actual last penny had already been spent by the time I crossed the threshold from ignorance into discovery. A little more money and I would have been fine; a little less time and I would never have known. The conjunction was the perfect agony. Everything I had ever wanted came just as, for the first time in my adult life, there was nothing I could do to grab hold of it.

5 REHABILITATION

Help came from a very surprising source. My father. After he had refused to help pay for my original treatment, one of the ideas which had been put to me in therapy was that I was simply setting myself up to be hurt over and over again by going back to him with my needs. This had in fact been exactly what had happened during the previous year. After I had lost and spent all of our money, I became increasingly frantic in my efforts to persuade him to help me. I came up with idea after idea, scheme after scheme, in order for him to underpin my life, bail me out and return some semblance of security back to my existence. In my panic I reasoned that this would make me feel safe again. In reality, the process of going back time and time again and always coming away with less than I felt I needed made me feel worse and worse. I could not see it clearly at the time, but it was becoming apparent now. So asking him for help was off the menu. I didn't even consider it.

There was another reason to be cautious. I felt that

he was, to some extent, complicit in the disaster of my finances, and therefore my life and therefore my health, but that this had remained totally unrecognised as part of our mutually destructive dynamic. In early 2008 he and my step-mother had taken my wife and I out for lunch and told us about a great investment he had made in a foreign oil venture which was imminently due to bestow upon him a very large return. As a result, they had decided to give enough money each to his three children – myself, my half-brother and half-sister, so that we could each have enough money to buy ourselves somewhere to live. This was a god send. My wife and I were really struggling to find a way of seeing a future in which we could balance our out-of-control domestic budget and were living in a rented house with our very young family. So this obviously seemed like a fantastic idea to us and was very much appreciated. We were given an estimate of a few weeks for the arrival of the money and were encouraged to use the early spring season to start house-hunting. We were wanting to move out of London anyway to find a cheaper way to raise our family and so we began our search.

In the end, the money never came. The African oil scheme surprisingly turned out to be too good to be true. However, unfortunately, with the prospect of a cash injection on top of a global economy which at the time was still bubbling over – seemingly infallibly after a decade of growth – I became even more reckless and risk positive in my deal making. We unwisely spent some of the equity in our Greek house which was supposed to underpin our loans there, but didn't recognise our own folly because this was how we had been living for a decade. At the time, though, it seemed that with the money we had borrowed being invested in property in surging economies in the UK and Greece, and with a cash windfall due any day from my father, nothing could possibly go wrong. I remember thinking that the absolute worst case scenario was that we would have to pay off all of our loans and just live in our small house in Greece. So we were very lucky because at least we would always have a home. A fatal assumption, alas. Over the next year or so it became apparent that all our leveraged property investments would evaporate, the expected underwriting windfall would never materialise, our only home would fall into negative equity and be repossessed, we would be left with more debt than we could ever pay, and that I had risked more than I could bear to lose. I ended up in the psychiatric hospital and my father ended up with his personal guarantee on my huge loans coming back to haunt him. Somehow we had conspired to facilitate each other to arrive at massively damaging outcomes when on the surface all we seemed to be trying to do was to help each other find some sense of security and a settled family life. So as I paused on the threshold of yet more treatment, avoiding my father and money seemed to me to be even more important than ever.

However, in the complicated triangle of conflicting emotions, my wife had asked him if he would pay for me to go to the trauma clinic and he had surprisingly agreed. It seemed that my new therapist's assertion that this treatment would restore me sufficiently to be able to work again was a powerful argument. I was astonished and left somewhat flummoxed. Frankly I wasn't sure how to feel or what to think. I had put a lot of emotional effort into accepting that I needed to run my life independently of his money and therefore had not even contemplated turning to him for help on this occasion, and yet it appeared to be the magic pill that I so desperately needed at that time. So I did not hesitate. I accepted the theoretical reservations about going back to that poisoned well for help, but for now all that mattered was that I was desperate. I thought I could recover and then deal with that problem. I was right, and I was wrong. More than anything I was just kicking the can further down the road, a road which I would have to return to time and time again, and for reasons that I would eventually come to see were much more damning than I ever would have wished to have known.

I returned to the UK for Christmas with my children as scheduled, arriving at our house just after lunch with my parents there too. I realised when I got home just how disabled and exhausted I was. It was lovely to see my family, but unfortunately I spent most of the next week in bed, completely wrung out and exhausted. I was able to talk to them a bit more than before and could join in with a few video games, but I was still very distant and preoccupied. They knew before I arrived that I was leaving again so perhaps it was hard to invest in really being together. And so, having worked out the funding for what I hoped would be the remainder of my treatment, I returned to the trauma clinic in Arizona a week later.

Within minutes of settling in, I knew that I was in the perfect environment for my recovery. Somehow, despite being a very basic facility, it felt safe. It was so different to the large busy hospital up the hill on the same campus. There was a tangible energy there which was completely new to me. It felt like the patients were actually doing something they valued. It was contained, being a U shape of buildings all facing inwards, and each of the two accommodation blocks had just four bedrooms, themselves all facing in towards a common sitting room. It was small, but snug and cosy; and the patients there were much, much less manic than at the clinic. I was surprised on arrival to find patients who had been there for nine months or more. Originally, on admission to the first clinic, I had been expecting to be fixed in just five weeks, a promise that was a legacy of something the rehab industry had spent decades routinely (and sometimes erroneously) doling out to the desperate from the early years of these kinds of 'sober houses'. The prospect of another four weeks at the clinic had, until that moment, seemed like something of a luxury. Now I began to wonder if it would be anything like enough time. Asking around, I got muted responses. "A good start," seemed to be the consensus. What on earth was I going to do if they failed to fix me in four weeks? For now, though, my sense of where I was was that I had died and gone to trauma heaven. For the first time in a year I was actually excited about my recovery, believed in the process to which I was giving myself over, and hopeful of a positive end result. Hanging over me always was the awful pressure as to how on earth I was going to be able to recover my external world and take care of my family, but at least for now I had a place to be and a way to get well. I tried my hardest to push those other problems further down the line and to make the most of my time in the present to investigate this mysterious process of 'healing trauma'.

I went straight into my first session and into a

therapeutic method called EMDR (eye movement desensitisation and reprocessing). This was a weird therapeutic modality which involved looking at some lights moving across a horizontal bar in front of me, listening to a sound alternately in my left and right ears and holding a buzzer in my left and right hand. They would co-ordinate so that the stimulation went from right to left and back again. This is known as bi-lateral stimulation. It is not really known exactly how this works, but it has been proved in record time by clinical trials to be very beneficial for a variety of the effects of what appears to be unresolved trauma. One theory is that it is a bit like simulating rapid-eye-movement sleep (REM) and therefore allows the brain to process things differently, like in a dream. All I remember about that first session was that the grinding sensation which had been trapped in my stomach since the end of the supposed trauma reduction course in the second week of my original treatment finally felt as though it had moved, and was at long last finding its way out. It had been ever-present for six weeks, making my life unmanageable, and now it was transforming into something else. It wasn't nirvana, but it was at least movement.

This was my first experience of what trauma therapists would call 'processing', or even 'discharge', the movement of neurobiological energy through the system, in the way that it was always intended to move by millions of years of evolution of our mammalian system. I knew nothing of this explanation of it at the time. To me it just felt like when you listen to a CD or watch a DVD which is stuck and torturing you by going round and round and round, making an incoherent, painful noise.

Suddenly the DVD was no longer stuck, and the story was starting to play again. I returned to an awareness of my mother's grief during the time that she was dying. I would have been between around four months and eleven months old and it seemed that I had absorbed much of her distress like a sponge. Moving some of it on was a huge relief, but this was also clearly just peeling away at the surface of what I needed to do. My therapist described my condition as 'over-coupled', which meant that many different traumas had become stimulated and seemed to have set each other off like a chain reaction. The result was like a nuclear bomb in my nervous system. Finally a therapist was telling me something which actually seemed to make sense of the way I felt. What is more, she was putting into practice the implied treatment and it was actually helping me. Day One was a result.

We did not just do trauma reduction (or processing) work at this trauma clinic. A huge part of our experience was being a member of the group of patients who were there and there was a method of working in a therapy group that was used to keep us a supportive community for each other. This was vital for preparing us to be able to do this deeper, very difficult work. We needed to feel safe in our new 'home'. This can be hard when a dozen or so highly reactive, overcharged, unwell individuals are crammed into a smallish living space. The way the trauma clinic staff kept us safe was with twice daily groups. They had devised a technique which allowed us to address anything we needed to about each other, but without offending or re-traumatising anyone in the process. On the whole it worked incredibly well. The basic premise was, "I can say anything I like about you so long as I am only talking about myself." There is, of course, an inherent paradox in this, but it brought staggering results on many levels and was referred to as a way of putting some limits, a boundary if you like, around the way that we talk – hence a 'talking boundary'.

It meant that I could be with someone with whom I was upset, perhaps even who I didn't like very much, and I was able to tell them how I was feeling, all the while both of us remaining completely safe and connected. There was an art to this communication and dialogue. It is the opposite of what most people with trauma routinely do in their lives, and is all about owning how one is feeling as opposed to blaming it on others. I took to it like a duck to water. I think my existing psychotherapy training helped, but certain analytical skills enabled me to understand its nuance quite quickly. It became the backbone of our community. If I had a problem with you, I had a new choice beyond my usual of keeping quiet, or attacking you. I could just let you know what was going on for me within the confines of this 'talking boundary'. I did not blame you, or require you to change, but just let you know who I was, in all my trauma, all my dysfunction and all my delusions, in response to what I thought I observed you doing or saying. It became much less important to pick up the other person on what they might (or might not) be doing wrong, and much more powerful simply to talk about what came up for me, to explain my experience from the 'I' position. This talking boundary became a staple of daily life and created a living environment more safe than any which I have ever known before or since. It was the perfect way to prepare a community for the arduous work of trauma treatment, but with all its rules, and the feelings of security in us to which these very rules gave rise, came a new, paradoxical desire in us, also, to make mischief.

In fact, mischief became one of our main medications against the pain and agony of treatment. There were many funny war stories from the other patients of former clients there who had made the transition from my kind of collapsed, infantile state into one resembling, more, a rebellious teenager energy. As I started to recover, I could feel this beginning to happen to me as well. I would go from being the wounded animal, to someone willing to fight back. I found my own particular outlet in the drama of the drainage pool and the labyrinth. There was this lovely stone labyrinth laid out on the desert floor next to our accommodation block. Sometimes we would walk it for hours just to keep the body moving. The stones traced a pattern on the earth and there was only one path in and out, so it was meant as a simple mediation rather than as any kind of maze. It is an ancient native American tradition from the area. During some rainy days, the campus' drainage pool, which was next to our labyrinth, became full. For some reason the maintenance staff would drain the pool with a pump and a hose onto the land next to our trauma clinic, invariably flooding our labyrinth. So every day we would sneak out early and lay the hose back around on itself so that it simply pumped the water back into the pond. And every day someone would fish it out again. It might not sound like much, but this was the first time for as long as I could remember that I was beginning to take action to change the world around me rather than just to give in to what was happening to me. I was saying 'no' to having our labyrinth flooded and doing so in the only way I had yet found possible. In time I would learn simply to express my disappointment and ask for what I needed directly but, at this stage of treatment, I was just waking up into the rebellion that characterises all of our first steps away from the despair of wounding and into a more active phase of recovery.

In this new environment, reconnecting with some of my own energy and desires, I was invited to start working on my over-coupled stack of trauma. With little time, no money and a conviction that this was the only possible treatment for me on the planet that had a hope in hell of working, I went at it with everything I had. We worked with two main trauma modalities, EMDR and Somatic Experiencing (which later would also be added to by Sensorimotor Psychotherapy). What they seemed to have in common was that they would both allow the middle part of the brain, (originally the mammal brain, now called the limbic system), to run the show and, in doing so, moved me on from my stuck places of looping in traumatic energy. Using these two methods in conjunction often had spectacular results since they would come at the problem in slightly different ways.

The caveat with all this work was that this processing had to happen inside 'something', a biological container of some sort, a metaphorical bowl, say, in which I carried all of my pain. I found that if that container was too small, weak or fragile, and I was to force it too full of my unprocessed traumatic energy, it could break or fracture and the result would be referred to as re-traumatisation. I came to understand that the entire set up of this trauma clinic, from the architecture to the language we used, from the rules and regulations to the timetable we adhered to, acted as a bigger bowl, lent to us by the institution during our treatment, a reinforcement for the busted personal container that I was trying to repair. Inside that nuclear bunker of protection, we could go farther, faster and deeper with this work than would ever have been possible in, for example, a weekly out-patient therapy. I hit the ground running, and then kept on going.

We started doing two EMDR sessions a week and they were extraordinary in their intensity. It was perhaps a combination of how much unprocessed trauma I had 'live' in my system, and also how safe I felt in that place, but the result were sessions which seemed to follow a chronological sequence of living out my life again from scratch. I continued to work through what appeared to be the overwhelming effect of taking on my mother's energy and emotions when she was dying. This was some of the hardest therapeutic work I have ever done. It simply felt like the scale of what I was carrying was cosmically beyond my ability to bear it. I didn't have many memories or flash-backs during these early sessions, but I could feel, unrestricted, the naked horror of my overwhelming emotions. Session after session was spent with my trying to 'clear' this channel, as they would call it.

The idea of EMDR is that you actually finish one of these stuck experiences, after which you feel completely different and emerge into a different sense of self and even reality. So, for example, I might get deeply immersed in some past experience, like watching my mother dying, but then once this had been 'processed', by feeling it without the normal resistance, I would be free of this sensation and notice that my mind and thinking would change. I might move from having a core belief such as 'everybody who loves me leaves me' to something like, 'I can sustain relationships with people'. Having finished the underlying energy trapped in the limbic system, my larger, more rational human brain is released into some more attractive ways of thinking. It might take a session, or in extremis perhaps half a dozen, to move on some traumatic energy, but it could not go on for ever; there simply was a finite amount of energy in the system to discharge. However, what I found was, just as one experience was coming to its closing stages, another one would come immediately after it, no let up, and I would be forced to start the process all over again, only with a new experience. This was the over-coupling which my therapist had been talking about and which had been making my symptoms so severe.

The processing of my mother's shock, terror and grief, which really was just allowing the body to 'feel' these pre-verbal sensations and emotions, took me back into the place in which I had been in the nurses' station after my first brush with the hospital's own trauma course. But this time I got to do it properly, slowly and guided by these expert, experienced professionals. For a week or two I was falling apart, but was also reassured by being held by therapists with an accurate understanding of my real problem. Far from being told to 'grow up', I was encouraged to know that this was nothing abnormal and gently and kindly supported through completing this phase of my treatment. In fact, at the very beginning, the only thing that made this whole process difficult was having to spend a session or two getting over the recent trauma of my treatment at the hospital! One of the tragedies of mental health treatment is that quite often the right treatment for the wrong problem can make things worse. This certainly had been my experience. I was astonished that two such different sets of expertise and different treatment modalities existed on the same campus just a hundred yards apart.

Perhaps one of the hardest moments came one day when I woke up not right at all. I could feel the worst excesses of my mental disintegration beginning to close back in on me. I struggled with it all day, worked with it in a session, spoke about it in group, but by the evening was starting seriously to decompose. I had a few Xanax in my medication cabinet left over from my days of hiding in the hospital, which I was reluctant ever to take, but began to think about just trying to numb out this awful sense of fragmentation and collapse. Instead I went to see the therapist who was about to start a meditation class and so was closing up for the evening. She was a true veteran of these battles. She looked at me with a rather long weary gaze and just asked me if I wanted to go to hospital. I said no, I wanted to get well and so she reassured me she would work with me, and cancelled the meditation class to do so. I was certainly a candidate for a hospital admission, no doubt, and any doctor in America or the UK would have been able quite reasonably to admit a patient presenting in the condition I was in. I was a barbequed mess of a mental patient, losing control and quite suicidal.

Instead, this woman asked me to pick up a squeezy child's toy, and massage it in my hand.

It was at times like this that doubt would creep into my hope for recovery. I was a grown man with a gilt edged academic education. I could understand science, theory, medicine even. I was clearly very unwell and getting quite unstable, and instead of taking what would have appeared to me to have been rational action, the woman was handing me a bright pink, luminous ball of rubbery goo. That was going to be my salvation? Maybe I had got this all wrong after all. There were other moments such as being asked to imagine being a bird flying down a mountain stream while we were in our therapy group, or the weirder extremes of art therapy propositions such as flinging clay at the wall and coming up with some meaning from the patterned residue. But I held the faith. Overall it was working, and so I followed her instructions and sat there squeezing a luridly coloured squashy toy, but was still stuck enough in my old ways to be asking her what possible good this could do me. She gave me the eyebrows and just told me to get on with it. The disconnect I felt between the scale of my problem and the banality of the solution really worried me, but I had nowhere to go, no other options, no better plan for myself.

Within about two or three minutes I was bawling my eyes out on the floor, curled up, wailing. As horrific as it was to be releasing this excessive scale of my mother's terrified adult's emotion from the tiny container of my infant, it was curiously better than feeling like I did before I had been able to do so. That simple trick of forcing me to connect with the sensation in my hands on that gooey, cold plastic, brought me out of my malfunctioning human brain and back into the natural process of my mammalian brain, one connected with sensation rather than thought. My limbic system had stuff to do and blocking it was making me both ill and crazy. It took a while to work through, but in less than half a regular session, this saviour of a woman had restored me to relative normality and I never had an episode this severe again.

I realised that the EMDR might be like taking an Exocet missile to the source of the stuck traumatic energy, but it was also important to let the system have time to integrate this in a more organic way. That is where the Somatic Experiencing (and Sensorimotor Psychotherapy too) came in, which is what the therapist was encouraging me to pull off by focusing on touch and sensation. It was probably my most dangerous moment in treatment, and her blasé skill, knowledge and confidence brought me though it in minutes. I could have been in a psychiatric hospital for a month, drugged up to the eyeballs. Instead, a little accurate treatment, based on some sound science (neuroscience and anatomy) and with a robust, seasoned practitioner had me sorted in no time. These were remarkable experiences for me to witness, thinking as I had before this illness that I was a pretty good psychotherapist back home. I began to realise that I knew nothing; that there was a new paradigm of recovery out there and that very few people seemed to be able to access it yet. Up the hill in the main hospital, they did not even know about this work which was going on under their very noses! It was genuinely exciting. It felt as if I was a pioneer, forging a new frontier, one of the first explorers to go into an exotic new territory, somewhere into which, over time, millions of people would follow me. My journey could even become one from which they might benefit. There was a sense of privilege, awe even.

But to arrive first myself, I would need help. I was running out of time and yet, because of the nature of what I was working with, I was, on the face of it, getting worse not better. There was simply no way that I could leave safely after only four weeks and it would have been a big mistake to have had to try. I was getting what I needed – finally – and could see that a full recovery was, indeed, possible, after all. But there was clearly so much more to do and no time left in which to do it. I remembered the muted responses to my original question to my fellow inmates when I arrived. Four weeks was actually hardly anything at all. "A good start," they had said and now I wholly took their point. The trouble was that I was so deep in my own process and fragile distress that I could not bear to attempt to negotiate with my father about further funding for my treatment. I left that to my therapist and for my part spoke only to my wife about it. She was unhappy and worried about yet another delay to my return. It was freezing cold at home and she had no money or help with our young children. She had been looking into cleaning jobs to make ends meet and just desperately wanted, and needed, her husband home. But I could not leave as I was. I knew what I needed too – in order, ultimately to become a better husband and father – and what I now had to do. And that this was the only place on earth that I could do it.

Unfortunately the news from London was negative. Either my father or my step-mother seemed underwhelmed by my therapist's explanations of my process and they were not inclined to pay any more to extend my treatment. My mind started to scramble. I thought of any and every person I had ever known who might be willing to help. My friend who I had been working for during the summer still owed me some money which he very generously had agreed to pay me upon terminating our contract together. I asked him for it, but he was reluctant to pay, having now, perhaps quite understandably, come to rather regret his largesse. I explained my circumstances but got no reply. I emailed a family member, someone who had been close to my mother and whose family was rich, hoping that sentiment would prevail, but he just referred me back to my father. I guess it is hard to see why someone should pay for the medical treatment of a man with a millionaire for a father. I was trapped and getting nowhere and this was not helping my treatment at all.

I firmly believed at that point that my life was on the line. In fact this was echoed by the clinical staff. They told me that if I had to leave they could not discharge me to the airport, by state law, given my condition. They would have to send me to a state psychiatric facility for three days before I could go home. I could only imagine what it was like in a state funded psychiatric hospital in Arizona, probably worse than prison. Wonderfully, generously, compassionately, my fellow patients one by one started to ask me if they could help. One middle-aged woman who was recovering from alcoholism and whom I had known for less than five days offered to pay for two weeks' more treatment for me. Another said that she could get her assistant to bring over an envelope of cash the next day to help. We were not allowed to lend or borrow money between us and yet I was sorely tempted, anything not to have to leave the one place on earth I most needed to be. The problem was that a week here or a week there didn't really cut it and, what was more, the anxiety of all of this drama was getting in the way of my remaining work which had actually been paid for. I needed a committed solution.

On the eve of my final paid-up week, my therapist was due to talk to my father in the morning, but told me that she was not expecting there to be any further help. She said I needed a miracle. I was devastated. I could not believe that my own family found it so hard to support me, to help me at such a critical point in my life. There was no doubt that I had exhausted their patience and generosity though my disastrous business dealings and bizarre behaviour, but I was still utterly baffled that they remained so unconcerned about my condition, given the reason why I had come to Arizona. I understood that it was very difficult for them to trust yet another professional, with yet another story of promised healing, with yet another eye-watering bill, and on top of that to trust me and the fact that I was making a good choice for myself when so many of my recent choices had seemed insane. So not only had I exhausted my own funds just when I needed them most, but also the goodwill of the people who could most easily help me and whom I thought would have the most motivation to do so. I understand now that it is a nightmare for families who are asked to pay for private mental health treatment. They simply don't know if it is necessary, do not fully understand what it is that they are actually buying, and what the consequences might be of doing so, or not doing so (if any). But at the time I was just utterly terrified, angry and heartbroken.

My friends had proved to be unhelpful, perhaps a product of my own selfish distance from them during the decade before, perhaps again a reflection of their perception of my family's own resources. And it seemed that extended family was disengaged for similar reasons. I was a prisoner of my own past mistakes, behaviour, wrong actions, and the presumption that if things really were that bad, my own father would automatically pick up such a bill that was, for him, very affordable. As it turned out, I had more support from relative strangers than from the people I had known half a lifetime. To top it all off, I had had an email from my wife saying that she was going to leave me if I wasn't better in a year, that she just couldn't take it anymore; I knew how she felt!

I predicted the scene that was bound to play out the following morning: receiving the inevitable news that I would have to leave that weekend. I wondered where that would take me. In my condition, I honestly could not imagine that I would survive for the three days confinement in a state hospital away from this enlightened treatment. To be this unwell, to know that I could recover but not to be able to get access to that treatment any more, to be in a very different psychiatric unit, locked up with even more of the truly desperate folk of Arizona, to be going home to a wife who had come to the very end of a very frayed tether, and to face a life without being able to work or being able to provide emotionally or financially for my children, was a mountain range I could not even contemplate let alone try to climb. I am not a coward, but I could not bear to face it. I could not see myself making it. I was barely a jot further on than when I started this pitiful journey, and had morbid notions of my own death being the only solution.

I thought about my father and his choices. I am quite sure he had many opinions to take on board and of course even he – who had opinions on many things – would not deny that he knew nothing about mental health treatment. But with the best will in the world, I just could not understand, having five children myself, how he could let such a plaintiff cry for help go unanswered by his first-born. Sure, I had already wasted a large sum of his money on my business fiascos, but compared to some of his own more fanciful business deals, the cost of this treatment was on a par with a nice lunch, and the prize at the end of it was his son's safe return to, stability and sanity. It just didn't make sense and, frankly, I worried for him that if I ended up a definitive catastrophe, of whatever sort, that he would regret this decision, in which case everyone would have lost everything for nothing.

So it was, I summoned up my courage and made one last attempt to enter back into that awful dynamic of pleading to him for his help. I wrote him an email that night. In it, I revised the story of my suicidal plans, my original need for hospitalisation and my need to remain in treatment at the trauma clinic. I explained that I was still at risk but would recover with my current treatment. I made sure he understood that, if I left now, I would not expect to become well again, and doubted that I would even make it home. I told him that I wanted him to be properly aware of all these things, although I had thought that he already had been, because I wanted him to be clear about what was at stake regarding whatever decision he chose to make the following morning. This was not emotional blackmail, but just the dark, raw, terrible truth; something which I had hidden even from my own wife. At the end of the email, I told him he was not, under any circumstances, to worry her even further with this information. And then I went to bed. And I prayed: a desperate, lonely, lost prayer, miles from the people I loved, stranded in the desert, unable to imagine the awful consequences of having to leave that facility the following day. My therapist was right. I did need a miracle.

With trepidation, I opened my email the next day. Nothing from my father. I was relieved that I did not have to deal with the gut wrenching anticipation of reading an email from him whilst so fearfully hoping not to be let down again. But I was in limbo. I didn't know if he had seen it or not, if the time difference had been a factor, or even if he was near a computer. Not knowing, however, was better than the certainty of a "no".

I did, though, have an email from my wife. This was further down my list of immediate priorities and frankly I had come to dread communication from her too, given her own pain and need for me to quit treatment, but I opened it anyway. It just said, "Is the email you sent to your father true?" The cat was out of the bag. He had of course completely disregarded my request not to tell her. I replied simply, "Yes, of course". I was in a new reality. I had kept my darkest thoughts from my wife to spare her the agony, the uncertainty, but now she knew. I picked up the phone to talk to her.

She told me that my father had no idea I was in hospital because I was suicidal. My step-mother had not told him, presumably not believing that I was serious. He was shocked and frightened by my email and had called my wife the moment he received it. I finally told her the whole story; about why I had left, why I didn't want to come back, how I had fought against my pain, minute by minute for the sake of our children, how I never wanted for them the fate I had suffered of growing up with a dead parent. She cried. I cried. Finally she said she completely understood and fully supported me. She said she would do whatever it took to keep me there and take care of the family while I healed. She also said that my father had agreed to pay for my treatment now for as long as it was needed. He had said on the phone to her that the only priority was to keep me safe for now. How I wept. I was safe. I was going to get well. I was going to return to my family a real man, a father, a husband, a provider. I was not, after all, going to rot in the guts of an Arizonian mental hospital, anonymous in the desert. The relief just flooded through my body and the tears kept coming. The other residents were stirring and found me outside on the phone. Concerned for me they checked I was alright, and I was fine. These were the tears of joy, of relief, of salvation. Finally, I was homeward bound.

The EMDR treatment continued and took a strangely linear pathway, seeming gradually to go forward in time from one stage to another. The problem was that there was no relief between these events. They were stacked like a pile of pancakes and, as soon as we progressed through one, another would surface. During the process, some new information and feelings emerged, things that would slowly make a lot more sense of my nervous breakdown.

I had begun with the sense of processing both my mother's and then my father's distress around the time of her death. I was able to move on through these pieces and to connect with my own grief, which seemed to feel very similar and yet different. These were subtle subjective experiences, and yet somehow it all seemed to become very clear. "The body knows" is one of this treatment's catchphrases and was repeated time and time again during our stay. This was ghastly work, dreadfully painful and searingly difficult to bear. However it was getting me better. I remember once being [cut] on one of our regular shopping trips in the local town and in the [cut] supermarket I bumped into one of the nurses from the original hospital. She was completely astonished at how I was walking around, fairly relaxed, shopping, joking, being relatively normal. She and her colleagues had known me only a couple of months before as one of the most severe patients they had ever had in treatment. What's more, I was only on a very slight dose of one simple medication; many people with less severe symptoms would be on a cocktail of drugs for years. This encounter made me recognise that my hard grind of allowing the passage of emotion and energy through my nervous system was paying dividends. Gradually, the excruciating intensity and activation of my nervous system was gaining some relief. My anxiety and general mood were, miraculously, experiencing some variation from the flat-lined misery which had been so consistent for so long. I found myself being playful occasionally, having fun, even laughing from time to time. This was a novelty indeed, something which I had forgotten as a possibility for well over a year. I was starting to recover.

The work went on and on, though, a dreadful grind from which I never shirked. I was so keen to get well and never knew when my treatment could be taken away from me, so every day was precious. One day the EMDR light bar machine was broken so I couldn't complete my session. I was very upset. These sessions were an absolute saviour, hard though they were, and I could not yet trust anyone else, anywhere else, to help me with this work. I just had to make the very best of it as quickly as I could.

Some very interesting material surfaced as I worked through the aftermath of my mother's death. During the last few months of her life, I had lived with her at her parents' house in Rhode Island. My father had been working in London and would make trips back to see us. After she died, I was left in America for a month before returning to England to go and live with a friend of my mother's, and her husband and little girl. So I never actually went home again to the house in Hampshire where my mother and I had lived since I was born, from where we moved to be with her parents at the end of her life. What came up in the EMDR sessions was how desperate I had been to go home after she had died, and my conviction, aged one, that if I could have just found a way to go home, then I would have been allowed to be with my mother again. Reflecting on my breakdown, the link now became clear. An obsession of mine as we lost all of our money was where my wife and children and I would live. I became convinced that we would never have a home again. I worried we would have to move out of our rented house, lose our house in Greece and become homeless with no clue about how to settle ever again. I found this to be a source of unbearable anxiety at the time, the prime motivator of my distress and even my suicidal thinking. It drove me again and again into despair, and seemed such an impossible hurdle to overcome. The very prospect of trying to build a home again for my family was, to my mind, an impossibility. It got to the point where I would have a terrible reaction to seeing estate agent signs advertising properties for sale. I could not read newspapers or magazines because of the adverts or articles about property. Towards the end, just driving around and seeing houses, whether mansions or much more modest terraces, would tip me over the edge. I just did not feel safe anywhere. The scale of my reaction to this otherwise manageable problem started to make sense, and then as more was revealed, so did my strategy for solving it.

I know that when I lived with my new family in England, my father would come to visit at weekends. I assumed that these would have been something which I had enjoyed. I had no reason to suppose otherwise. But what emerged in these sessions was my absolute desperation for him to take me with him. Again my fantasy was that he could take me home to my mother. I was less than eighteen months old and could not talk, but I guess I could long for my actual family and was sentient enough by that age to be able to associate my father with my mother and home. I was in screaming agony when he would not take me home. This appeared to fit very neatly with my more than usually anxious adult desire to be securely settled in a stable home of my own. I became obsessed with finding any way I could to encourage my father to help me to have one. Ideally I wanted him to buy me one, which I could then live in safely forever with my own family, but this was very expensive and I had already been wholly responsible for him losing a huge amount of money. So it seemed like the most absurd request of all time, supremely grabby and spoilt, and yet I was absolutely inconsolable without it.

I couldn't understand why I was so fixated on him solving my problem for me. Perhaps it had a sort of logic. After all he was my father, he had the money to do so and was therefore, possibly, my best chance. But, equally, disproportionate longing and fatal vulnerability seemed to outweigh the logic by far. Other grown men do not continue to look to their fathers for financial assistance, beyond perhaps the absolutely necessary. Whatever, I couldn't stop it and the only way I thought I would ever be sane again was to win this pitiful argument with him for more help. It reached the point where I even begged him to sell one of his houses and buy me the comparatively inexpensive house we were renting, which was for sale. I remember telling him he was "cruel" when he refused. In truth, if that had really been the answer to ending my suffering, his response could have been construed as cruel, but inevitably we were seeing different problems. My real one was now being revealed in my trauma work. As a baby, I had wanted him to take me 'home', back to my mother, and that need, that child-like pent up energy, had never left my nervous system. This present loss of a house had taken me right back to my infancy, brought up feelings with which I could not cope or contain and which I could no more bear as an adult than I had been able to as a baby.

I began to wonder again about the story of my childhood – the nice soft landing on to this loving surrogate family, punctuated by tender visits from my father, giving way to our own new family life with his new wife. In the end, via the modern miracle of the internet, I contacted that little girl with whom I had lived for two years. I have no memories of living with that family at all, but she remembered my sojourn there well. She recalled those "terrible visits from your dad, how scared you were at first and then how happy, and then how you screamed and screamed when he left, and were even more withdrawn and sad afterwards." I had never heard this version of events but it fitted perfectly with what I had experienced in those EMDR sessions.

It is easy, I suppose, to doubt what comes up in some odd, little understood, quasi-hypnotic treatment dished out by fancy therapists in the desert for a handsome fee. It's not really surprising that many people find that cynicism about these things comes very easily, and faith in them is hard won. Perhaps this is sometimes valid. I was struck, though, how accurately this woman's recollections seemed independently to validate my experiences in therapy. What came up for me in EMDR was a total surprise to me, and yet tallied perfectly with her recollections of the same event, all totally new information for me. I had never, ever been told by anyone that there had ever been anything negative about my father's interaction with me when I was staying with that family. I had no reason to think that nor any desire for it to be true. Having glimpsed this though in EMDR, I could see, of course, how it made perfect sense.

These memories of my childhood friend – recalling how scared I was, then how happy, then how I screamed and screamed when my father left before collapsing again – were exactly the same as those which had come up in EMDR; and also exactly what I had unwittingly re-enacted in the year before I went into hospital. I had each time been terrified to ask my father for help, then worked up great hope and expectation when he connected with me to talk about it, only to be utterly, inconsolably heartbroken when he turned me down again. The trauma was repeating itself, which was why I became so ill. At the trauma clinic they were completing these experiences for me, which was why I was improving so dramatically. The EMDR seemed to break through these barriers and the Somatic Experiencing would then settle them down. It was a compelling and powerful combination.

This phase of revisiting my childhood through treatment concluded with reliving the experience of my eventual return to my father. Aged around two, I went to live with him and his new wife. It seems that, on one level, I again had high hopes as I embarked on that transition, but all I discovered in EMDR was the devastation of realising that I had been moved to the wrong home and the wrong mother. This was as hard a part of the journey as any. It perhaps marked the start of my 'normal life' as a child and, in truth, there was a great deal more stability for me after this time, but perhaps it also marked the end of that baby's hope of returning to the life he had once enjoyed. Like an orphan, constantly hoping to be chosen, to be taken to a loving home, I had clung on to the vain hope that there would be a reversal for me, a return to Avalon, where my mother and I would be again as one, at home, happy and safe.

This now seemed to be a forlorn hope. The crushing blow of finally returning to my father, but finding him in the wrong house with the wrong woman, left me with no tether left back to my mother, no active fantasy about how I might recover her, or who would take me to her. I think that these longings must have been driven deep into the unconscious at that point and been left there for every woman I have ever known to endure. I spent my life searching for that attachment to the perfect feminine ideal, making me both intriguing to women, but also endlessly punishing; no-one, inevitably, could be good enough, no step-mother, surrogate carer, friend or lover, no amount of energy or good intention could satisfy me, without treatment for this long-forgotten, buried part of me. Something had clearly shifted at this point in my childhood and, in turn as I processed it, something moved in my adult recovery. It was at this point that my trusted therapists chose to recommend that I might go home and find a therapist there to continue this work with me. It seemed as good a moment as any.

However, one strand was left untied. During this phase of treatment, a single session had popped up as an outlier in this clear, logical, linear journey through the revisiting of my early childhood. Somewhere around the time of my mother's death, or after as I was being moved from house to house, I was propelled into a very dark sense of ominous threat. As I sat there in the chair, tunnelling deeper into my EMDR-induced return to the past, I had the oddest sense that I was clothed in the exact inverse of a man in a pair of underpants. I seemed to be naked exactly where my pants should have been. As I sat on the chair, I squirmed and squirmed, uncomfortable, unclear, unsafe. All I could identify was this weird sense of sexual vulnerability and nakedness. Nothing more was coming up and, for all the trouble that I was having at the time, I don't think that I wanted it to either. The session ended unresolved, but with me carrying away my anxieties and worries about it. Fortunately, it was quickly replaced by other work and I never did revisit it. What it meant I would not know until much later.

Its secrets would reveal the deepest layer of the provenance of my distress and finally lay bare the whole road map of the disastrous trail of my life, its dynamics and my choices. The real force behind my many crises revealed a truth which no child would ever wish to know about him or herself. But it was as that hideous truth finally came to light that I was at last able to let go of my terrible shame. The revelation of what had been done to me – as opposed to by me – meant that, all along, I had had very little choice as to how this story was going to pan out.

7 REDEMPTION

I emerged from my sojourn in the desert to some extent all shiny and new. I passed through the doors from customs into the arrivals hall at Heathrow on a sunny March morning. My wife and five beautiful children were there waiting for me. As I received their various hugs, I realised that I was 'with' them for the first time in well over a year and for the first time ever with my youngest.

They were so bright, loving and full of life. It was the greatest of joys just to be able to sit still with them, to look at them while they were talking, to listen to them, to play with them. I remember we played catch there and then with a baseball I had bought for them as a present, just talking and playing like children were supposed to do with their dad. It took us an hour to even get out of the arrivals hall. No-one wanted to go anywhere in case we would jinx it, lose this magic moment, wake up and find out that it was all just a dream. I was home and I wasn't leaving again. The worst of the storm was over but now we had real life to wrestle with.

I was no longer mentally ill, but I was far from fully recovered. It is fair to say that they saved my life with the medication at the hospital and the treatment at the trauma clinic but this only gave me a new problem to solve. There is a point in recovery which can be a difficult one, depending on an individual's circumstances, which I began to cross. Instead of measuring each day by how far away I was from the bottom of my life – which in my case meant how suicidal I didn't feel – I started to look at it in terms of how far away I was from the peak experiences of my life, which was now pretty bloody far ! My wife and I still had barely any money left and no sign of any coming in. We were temporarily settled in a rented house outside Oxford and the children were happy enough in their new schools. I was being pursued for various debts of which I couldn't pay a single penny. I still needed a lot of treatment, which was going to cost my father even more money which he was starting to question again. I had no work, no job and probably no career either. I also had numerous bridges to build at home, with an exhausted wife and pretty freaked out children.

Slowly the stories of their winter began to be told and were in places extremely hard to hear. My wife had been called in to see the nursery teacher of our three year old daughter who had explained that she had been overhead telling other children that her daddy was dead. All the children seemed overjoyed to see me, but I could see in the shock on all their faces that it had been a long haul. They would do things like come and climb into bed with me in the morning and just lie there next to me while I slept. It would take a long time for the scars of the preceding months – and indeed the year before that – to heal, but what everyone had told me in treatment was right: the best thing I could have ever done for them was to have stayed in hospital, recovered myself, and dealt with the familial fallout later. The children had their father back, and he was not dead. That's why I had gone away and it had worked. Someone, somewhere had known what to do. The rest we could deal with later.

With time on my hands, I started to think about the treatment that I had had in the UK, both from the National Health Service and privately. My first response to this was just anger. How could so little help have been on offer and how could the little that I did get have gone so wrong? Why didn't the British medical profession know about what they were doing in America? Why wasn't this 'miracle' cure, which I had stumbled upon by chance thousands of miles away from home, available here? What on earth were the NHS and those private doctors doing?

Like some people who get angry, I decided to do something about it and I was lucky to have the perfect vehicle through which to do so. Before I had lost my mind, I had been asked by a local think tank to head up a commission into mental health. By the time it got going I was very unwell and it had fallen to the very bottom of my list of worries. Now that I was back, I went to see its chair and told her all about my marvellous mystery tour. I probably thought that I was doing very well at the time given how I had been a few months before but, looking back on it, I am sure I came across as a bit bonkers compared to normal, functioning folk. I was still somewhat overwrought, continuing my trauma therapy and slightly agitated by my medication. I was probably also a bit manic and messianic, not perhaps the most settling of combinations. Nonetheless, I was convinced that I had an urgent mission to tell her and her colleagues all about this exciting world that they were yet to discover. I assumed that since they were reporting on the state of the nation for mental health treatment in the UK, they would be interested in news of something which actually seemed to work. I could not have been more wrong.

Eventually I inveigled my way into the commission working group and gave them my own evidence deriving from my experiences both as a sufferer and in treatment. I even prepared for them a summary from a questionnaire which I had done with seven fellow patients at the trauma clinic, just to show that I wasn't an isolated case. I wished also to convey the extent to which other people believed in these methods for, unanimously, they reported that this treatment had saved their lives following a long history of failed treatments elsewhere. Unfortunately I had not yet been briefed on the state of the politics of mental health treatment in the UK. It turned out that there was far more at stake here than the simple matter of getting helpless people well. This became a refrain that I would hear throughout the UK and in other countries too: reputations, careers, academic positions, research grants, university status and profit were all much more important in the end to the people who made the decisions than the reality of one lost person for whom treatment was never going to work.

One of the key professors running this show for the government was on our working group. He was as impressive as an academic and a politician could be, like a cross between Einstein and Tony Blair, but singularly unimpressed by my story, laughing with a colleague, in front of me, that "the plural of anecdote is not evidence." There was no engagement at all. I was shocked. Much later I would have a dinner with one of his senior colleagues who argued with me that their system of delivering mental health treatment in the UK, which they had designed and was predicated originally almost exclusively on CBT, worked. When I asked this man then how come it nearly killed me, he simply replied that I had been "unlucky". The statistical approach to mental health treatment I could understand but, drowned out in this mudslide of managed evidence and the hundreds of millions of pounds of public money which it funnelled into some very narrow treatment modalities in the UK, were the voices of the ordinary people who routinely slipped through the net. I had been one of them and, on their behalf, I determined to give these voices a platform.

I was fortunate to find a practitioner of Somatic Experiencing who had just moved back to the UK from Canada and had been one of the first people to train in the method. She was not at that point too busy yet, so I was able to have two precious sessions a week with her in order to continue my treatment. From her perspective, I was highly agitated still and it took months to help bring me in to land following my inordinately intense ten weeks at the trauma clinic. I should have been there longer and taken that treatment more slowly, but I had no choice other than to take every chance I had had to get on with it while I had someone paying for me. This process itself now needed some recovery, which was an interesting and slower process. Going at this steadier rate was like paying attention to a detailed repair job to a wall that had been blasted clean. I often used to think of EMDR as the sandblaster and SE as the delicate brush with which we would clean up the surface afterwards. The goal was a smooth, shiny finish, and just like on a real wall, every subsequent layer of finishing work was more delicate, intricate and careful than the previous one. I managed to go over the material from before again, sometimes in a more random way, but with more time, care and softness in my system. Much of the emotion was yet to resolve itself. I would spend months grieving before moving on to a deeper resolution of the whole system.

One of the odder features of deep nervous system recovery is the twitching, shaking and trembling which all mammals appear to experience as the sympathetic nervous system discharges. One day I started twitching furiously in my session. As the session ended, I stopped. It did not happen again until I walked up the path to my therapist's door when it would immediately start again! This happened for weeks. With every passing iteration, my nervous system was calming down and I was beginning to resemble nothing more uncommon than a rather stressed out normal person. I was able to come off my medication – a bit of a drama in its own right but I managed it – and survived the ups and downs and anxieties which this created. I ended up unmedicated, stable, sleeping, able to have fun, play with my children, relate to my wife and even begin to become professionally productive again.

Without this treatment, I could have been a

burden to the state for ever, but I was getting ready to be able to work again. I could not let go of my interest in why the state could not provide such treatments more successfully and, also, my entrepreneurial instincts started to kick in, thinking that if these treatments really were so untried and untested in the UK that this represented an opportunity to bring something really valuable to the private sector too. Strangely, at the same time, a number of surprising opportunities came my way for me to reflect that reality back to the very system which had failed me. I just kept showing up for things and opening my mouth and riding the waves to wherever they happened to deposit me. And that just kept getting better and better.

And so just over a year after I had left treatment, and through nothing much more than my enthusiasm for finding out who had let me down in my original quest for treatment and trying to bring them to account, I found myself at a dinner in Westminster which was being arranged as a forum for discussing new psychological treatments and new ways to get them to the public. I had worked hard with the think tank to come up with some useful new policy ideas and also set up a not-for-profit social enterprise which could deliver on these ideas. My nascent organisation was now the 'host' of a dinner for about twenty various ministers and officials from the new government and the American pioneers who devised the treatment which I had received at the trauma clinic, who were over in the UK for a conference. The goal was to try to promote the use by the National Health Service of a wider range of therapies, such as the ones which I had been lucky enough to stumble upon in the desert. I have no idea if the dinner was a productive use of anyone's time, but for government officials to hear about the latest thinking in treatment could only have been helpful. For me, it was just a moment to savour. My recent passion for lobbying for better treatment for those who could not speak for themselves collided wonderfully with my private passion and fascination for the icons of the American therapy world who had made this happen. I had the privilege of being able to thank them in person that evening; a wonderful coda to my experiences in Arizona.

The sad part though was that as I observed everyone at that dinner, I saw the contrast between their lives and my own. I noticed how much more calm and capable many of the senior people were than me. Obviously, they do these things all the time but, in a way, that was the point. Their demeanours had an ease about them which mine lacked. I felt that this was because they had followed a more traditional path – that of improving their careers and their skills and in turn their very existence. Mine had cycled, going nowhere, since my mid-twenties, and the main and enduring reason for that was that I had been plagued by anxiety and fear. This was now getting properly treated, finally, but it was extraordinarily tenacious and something was still holding me back. If I was going to flourish in any career, I would have to move beyond it. If I was going to recover as a human being, I would have to put it behind me. What 'it' was, was still not entirely clear. There was a level at which my system had recovered, but then come to a grinding halt. I needed to let something else go and, yet after nearly a year and a half of this trauma work, I was still hiding something from myself, something which would finally unlock much of the mystery of my bizarre life choices, and open the door for me to a final resolution for my nervous system. When I found it, of course in many ways I wished I hadn't, and I understood why I had spent so much time in treatment avoiding it.

At some point in my on-going trauma therapy in a little house in South West London, I started to get odd sensations in my body. I could feel pain and blockages of energy which would give way to experiences of pain in my rectum. Every time this happened, I was reluctant even to report it to my therapist. It seemed both shameful and something I did not want to acknowledge. However, I knew enough by now to accept that if I wanted to get well I had to follow the clues of the body and that there was work to be done here. This is often every patient's dilemma in therapy: the desire to repress versus the need to move on. I was guilty of that in spades.

This was the third time this had come up for me in my therapy history. First was in my twenties, when I was having therapy with a wonderful woman in north London for panic attacks. We stumbled upon a very odd reaction I had to my wife talking about how Mediterranean woman would change male babies' nappies, and her describing how amazingly unabashed and playful they were about the dramas that would ensue from an unfettered baby's private parts. It made me feel incredibly uncomfortable. I also noted that I found stories of paedophiles in the news very hard to bear and would become angrier reading them than I would about anything else. I remember I even allowed myself the luxury of a private opinion that the death penalty was justified for this crime, if for none other. I am not an advocate of the death penalty and never have been, even, intellectually, for paedophiles. It was a horrid, uncomfortable but instinctive feeling and made me tussle with my conscience. My therapist at that time had been pragmatic, warning me against the danger of over-reacting to this kind of thing and coming up with thoughts about any abuse as a child which may not have been accurate. This seemed like sensible advice.

The second time this possible theme of some kind of sexual history to my trauma had come up was in that EMDR session in Arizona when I felt very creepily exposed, threatened and violated. Given that my every other experience in EMDR seemed to correspond exactly with the truth of my life, some of which was also independently validated afterwards – my fathers "terrible" visits, for example – this only gave rise to a further worry about what had actually gone on in my childhood. Now, this was the third time this had come up in therapy in my adult life. I was having what we call 'body memories', which appear to be the deeply repressed actual sensations from physical abuse being recovered, processed and released, which of course is excruciatingly uncomfortable. These are, unfortunately, commonly seen during nervous system work on people who were the confirmed victims of sexual abuse in childhood. I seemed to be no different to them. What could possibly have happened?

Eventually, I did gather up the courage to work through some of this material. My therapist never pushed it, never once suggested it to me or interpreted it for me. Unfortunately she left it to me to bear the horror of giving words to what my body was telling me. Working through the sensations and letting go of some of the energy around them was helping me to move into a new phase of recovery. But I was clearly stuck at something. I had no knowledge of what had happened, no information. Sometimes people might have their own stories to complement this material – memories, or shared knowledge in the family, school or community – as it emerges. I had nothing. I had been at boarding school for ten years and perved on by the deputy head master when I was twelve in a creepy way, but nothing seriously illegal had happened. And anyway this material was all coming from much further back. I remembered the chronology in EMDR. It fit with the sense of self I had when these sensations came up. This was something which had happened around the time after my mother's death; a time I had no memories of whatsoever. So round and round I went, unable quite to clear this material, but taking it slowly, giving it time to do whatever it needed to do. My hope (and this is possible, but more difficult) was that it would simply resolve itself in my system without my ever needing to know what exactly had happened. And yet somehow I was still stuck, hovering on the threshold of a deeper knowing, a knowledge that I would have given anything, except it seemed my life, to be spared.

Finally, one session, months and months into this work, I was deep in the experience of trying to process this through the body by staying with the painful body sensations – general aches and specific pains from those body memories – as they would present themselves, an awful place to be and one I had grown sick of struggling with. I was more than anxious to move on, to escape. I complained of my weariness. My therapist said that sometimes it helps people when they have some sense of what has happened, any memory or flashback, because this can help to complete the cycle, but I had had none. So she let it go, but just as I was giving into despair about ever coming through this piece, my father randomly popped into my head. My father. What was he doing there? Why would I think of my father as I was struggling through this terrible place of abuse. Then the worst thought of all stuck me, instantly dismissed. Why was my father 'here' as I was recovering from being sexually abused? Why was he here? What was he doing?

What was he doing?!?

I did not want to say anything out loud. I wanted to just put that out of my mind, to file it, to put it down to a random thought only, an unrelated association. A reaching out for something safe during a time of crisis, perhaps? I kept it to myself, horrified, frozen, yet knowing that this was something I needed to share. I was caught between the threshold of two realities, two competing versions of the universe. Eventually I told my therapist that I had been thinking about my father, who had spontaneously popped into my mind. She asked me simply what that meant for me. I wasn't sure. And yet I was. My brain was saying "no" and yet my body was relaxed. The mammal's nervous system, our 'limbic system' carries no social mores, no stigma, no judgement or societal values. Mine at that moment was just relieved to be able to let go of something I had been carrying inside me for my whole life, something which had wound my system up to the max. But my head was not going to let this happen. I had no interest or appetite for linking my father even to the idea of sexual abuse, let alone the possibility of him having done that to me. That was not going to happen. It was impossible for anyone who knew him to imagine that of him, just impossible. He just didn't seem the type; a decent, diligent man, with a successful career both in business and sport, a family man, a good friend, husband and father. There was no way, on the surface of it, to lend this idea any credibility at all.

And yet something very profound did happen after that day: I relaxed. There has been a lot of controversy about 'recovered memories' in therapy, centred around exactly this kind of thing, with passionate and heartbroken proponents on both sides of the debate. I do not know about any of those cases, or much about the syndrome that goes with it, but I was able to examine my own. I asked my therapist if there could really be any truth at all in this. In turn, she asked me just to consider two questions. First, had this ever been suggested to me by her or anyone else? And the answer was truthfully, no. (In fact, I would have been outraged). Second, once I had allowed the possibility of this information to become part of my reality, did my system calm down? And the answer was emphatically yes, yes, yes. Therefore, from an empirical place of clinical logic, theory and experience, sadly, she would conclude that it was most likely that my father had indeed been the person who raped me.

This was utter madness, and I could not, would not accept it. What possible justification could there be for this wild and unfounded accusation? That just wasn't a world which I wanted to be a part of. But I did have to admit, as shocked as I was, I had never felt calmer, more settled, more 'regulated' even, in my body, in my nervous system, and in myself. Could this possibly dare to be the truth? And if so, how could I possibly find out? I wanted to know more, but I absolutely could not talk about it either. For all my openness and honesty, for all the stories I have shared with others – with my unflinching determination to declare to the world the horror of untreated mental distress – my evolving doubts about my father remained my own. I dismissed them at source. It wasn't that I wasn't willing to share them with others; I was unwilling to share them even with myself.

It was of course too private, too unfair, too uncertain to talk about. And also just too awful. But more than that, it was also something that had always been too risky for my psyche ever to allow itself to bring to light. As a child, with my mother dead, my attachment to my father was absolute. I always deeply loved him and regarded him as the only point of safety in my life. If he had in fact been my rapist, this would have set up a terrible double bind, where the point of ultimate safety and ultimate threat in my life would have converged. It is like a rabbit running to his burrow when the alarm is raised that there is a fox in the field, only to find when he gets near the hole that the fox is standing over it. The rabbit's instincts come unstuck. There is no biological way to solve the problem, the nerves firing both for forward and in reverse simultaneously. This would have been a disaster for my nervous system which would have been off the chart with an activated response to threat. I needed this man. He was my only remaining family. The result is a nervous system which is out of control with no capacity to correctly 'regulate', a mind which becomes fragmented into different parts, unable to bear all of reality in one place at one time.

To run away from the only person on earth who I could have reasonably expected to keep me safe I would have had to risk everything. My father was my one link to my mother, my only immediate family member throughout most of my life. It was impossible as a child to have imagined giving that up. Far easier, surely, would have been just to bury that memory and all of the frozen energy which went with it, to separate my truth, and my life, into a private dungeon of danger and a present fantasy of security. This illusory separation of danger from security was a kind of structural separation of myself into at least two completely separate Benjamins, and this then became the cornerstone of my poor relationship with reality, and later my poor mental health, in my life from then on.

As a child, the prevailing pretence in our household was that my step-mother was my mother, and I always believed this to be the case. And I also knew it wasn't. It became clear in my EMDR that when I met my step-mother, I knew she was the 'wrong' mother and also I remember, aged four or five, asking why I had three grandmothers and being told the whole story. So I knew, and yet I didn't. That was not the reality I lived in. My own mother was never openly referred to in our family and I took advantage of that to find myself a new identity. It seems that I became deeply split, putting the 'bad' stuff of my first two or three years into an alternative reality and investing fully in living in the life that followed, our mutual fantasy of the happy nuclear family.

This habit never left me and throughout my adult life friends and family would often say that I was living in a "dream land". I see now that I most definitely was. The madness of the way that I was living before my breakdown, and the fact that I thought that it might be ok, shows just how far gone I was. When 'reality' became no longer avoidable (and lack of money is often the ultimate reality check), I just fell apart. The scaffolding of my highly compartmentalised internal world shattered and I did so with it. I was beginning to see that the genesis of this splitting of myself into two (or more) realities may not have been, as I had always assumed, my new family's reluctance to remember my real mother, but may in fact have been the events that led me to become two completely separate different people long before I even met my step-mother; the part of me that seemed to know that my father had raped me, and the part that could never know. The task I faced in treatment was to start to accept the reality of both of these parts of myself and to integrate them. This would allow me, finally, to recover both my health and my ability to live in the real world.

However, returning, as an adult, to face the possibility of an acceptance of such a difficult truth has been agonisingly difficult. I am sure there may have been people who have made up such allegations, or wantonly embellished the truth for their own reasons – perhaps to make excuses for indefinable pain, or for vengeance, or any manner of things, but I was sure that I could never be one of them. There is nothing I would rather disbelieve than that my father raped me. For so many reasons but not least for my own sense of honour, to avoid the horror of the most intimate experience of shame, and because of my deep need to invest in and maintain the love I sincerely feel for my father. Really, who would want that to be true? The idea that it appeared to be him who ruined my life, the one person who had sustained it for over forty years, left me inconsolable. And yet to hide from it, and to hide it from the world, would be to collaborate with the crazy-making, personality splitting, reality deceiving madness which had plagued me my whole life long. It was a terrible choice to face.

In the end, there was only one way to go. Hiding from what my body had to say had made me ill to the point of destruction. The way back was a linear path. In accepting what my body seemed to be telling me, I came to understand the extraordinary events of the last few years in a new and enlightened way. My nervous system all along, it seemed, knew what it was up to. In an amazing series of coincidences and bad judgements, I had managed to turn myself from an independent and successful business man into a bankrupt and broken infant, and in doing so render myself vulnerable to the one man that I most needed to come to know more clearly. I had perfectly recreated my childhood; a cataclysm of seeming total loss, followed by repeated desperate attempts to get my father to rescue me. In doing so, I set him up to say "no" to me over and over again, refusing to take me "home" and bringing me right into the very dynamic which appeared to have resulted in my most traumatic injuries of all. I had pointed my life squarely at the path of 'trauma repetition', something which I now understand is the fate of every unresolved nervous system.

Stored in my nervous system was the perceived knowledge of my father's abuse of me, buried, occluded, defended against. My cognitive mind might never wish this to see the light of day, but my deeper mammal brain had other ideas. This kind of traumatic energy is harmful to the nervous system, resulting in the kinds of symptoms which eventually hospitalised me. But also on a more benign level, it directed my thinking, relationships and behaviour, never as I wished them to go, but always in a way which gave me a chance to 'wake up' this material, which was so deeply frozen and ignored. Of course, in the process, I would destroy myself and make myself vulnerable to the one person whose abuse of me I most needed to address in order to recover my biological health. It is what we all do. We run the patterns of our lives over and over again, always baffling our conscious minds, because we end up with the opposite of what we are aiming at, but while doing so, we give ourselves a chance to resolve the original incident. Unfortunately for human beings, this rarely seems to work without some expert guidance, at least not when the injury is very severe. But that doesn't stop millions of years of evolution guiding us to keep on trying.

Seeing how my life had played out in a perfect ballet of trauma repetition finally gave my experience meaning. Everything now made more sense. Nothing was comfortable or pleasant to live with, but chaos had been replaced with order. I realised that I wasn't crazy at all. I was in fact quite normal – for a mammal.

This awareness of what my body seemed to be

telling me gave me back a life which I thought was over for ever. When I recognised that, everything began to make sense and I no longer felt solely responsible for how I had been. For example, it suddenly seemed crystal clear to me what my father and I had been doing with money as adults. Two grown men, good at business, capable with money, had conspired to bring about something catastrophic (not to mention almost moronic) for each. Now I saw that it could make sense. Perhaps we had played out our respective guilt and rage through this arrangement. I had sabotaged myself so that I could go back to that early place of needing him, to revisit that unhealthy relationship dynamic, and he had once again failed to give me that which I was seeking, which of course was everything; I needed too much and he could only give too little. But in the revisiting, I got to have my revenge, and he got to pay. In an odd, awful, destructive way, we both got what we needed. And both ended up with nothing. This had not been therapeutic, or helpful. It was trauma repetition, not resolution. Until my body got the help it needed to finally make use of this awful drama.

It was a huge relief to me to be able to see my life from three hundred and sixty degrees. Everything at long last made sense. I shed a huge load of self-loathing, shame and despair. It no longer seemed as if I was an accident waiting to happen, about which I couldn't do anything. I was beginning to make sense of me, and this meant that I might have a choice over how to be and what would happen in my life. It was also terrifying to see how damaging the consequences of all of this had been. I had destroyed my family's financial security, robbed my wife and children of comfortable, secure lives with an easy future, and all just to act out a wicked Oedipal drama with my father – armed with all the strength and weapons of an adult, but driven by all the madness, rage and lack of control of an infant. Of course I had burnt the house down, and in doing so had taken with me everyone that I most dearly loved. This is the tragedy of damage. Pain begets pain begets pain. If we don't do something successful and informed about it, then it can cycle through the generations for ever. I saw that I needed to do something. It was time to rebuild.

The therapy was one thing. This internal work was vital, the foundation stone of change, but also I needed to get a life. I had a large family to feed and few options. The one thing I knew how to do was to start things and through my treatment I had come face to face with game changing innovation in this area of health care. It seemed like an opportunity waiting to happen for me, but battered and broke I had no idea how to go about lifting this heavy, weary, doubtful phoenix from the bonfire of my devastated life. And then, just as things were changing on this inside, things started to happen around me on the outside too.

One of the consequences of attending that dinner about these new paradigms of treatment in Westminster was that it stimulated me to write an article in the Times about my experiences of treatment in America. The article was perhaps a two thousand word version of this book, explaining in some detail my own story and attempting to help more people to know that newer, better, more effective treatments were on their way. I concluded it by offering the personal whimsy that it was a fond dream of mine one day to set up such a clinic. The response to the article was extraordinary. I received hundreds of emails from people who could directly relate to my story. I was not alone in harbouring a sense of frustration and alarm at the failure of both state and private mental health treatments, particularly for quite severe disorders. The lovely thing was that along with the many requests for help, as well as the validations of my own disastrous experience, were others who asked me how they could join in my quest to make a difference and make things better. A standout among these was from a reader who said that she had a house we could use for starting a treatment centre. She had leased it in order to establish something similar herself but had never quite got it off the ground and wondered if I would like to use it!

I was astonished. I had set up a number of businesses in my twenties and thirties, restaurants, night-clubs and hotels, and in each case, no matter how brilliant the concept was, how secure the funding, how strong the team, the one immutable difficulty which would make or break the actual realisation of the project was a property. I had not imagined it would be any easier finding one for a treatment centre than it had been finding one for a nightclub. Although property is perhaps the most prosaic item on the shopping list for a treatment centre, the quality of the building, its layout, location and, often most importantly, the cost, are a huge factor in settling down all the other elements required to make something like this work. This woman seemed to have done all of this hard work for me and was handing it to me on a plate. Frankly, I hadn't expected to do anything like this for some time and it was very early in my recovery to be taking on such a task, but it was also just so tantalising. I agreed to meet her and to see the property.

It was a huge, modernised, private house two hours north of London, like the kind in which you might imagine a footballer would live, with grounds, a pool and large individual bedrooms each with their own bathroom. There was an annex where the therapeutic work could take place. In short, it was ideal: already rented for the purpose and sitting there empty, ready to go. I have never been one to look a gift horse in the mouth and so this was a hard opportunity from which to walk away. Meanwhile, some of the people who had contacted me for help wanted to know when I would be setting up this clinic because they wanted treatment as soon as possible. It seemed to me that, simultaneously, I was being offered a property which I could not have hoped to secure on my own and ready-made clients, whom I would never have expected to come my way so easily. After nearly two years of doing not much other than some infrequent and unpaid lobbying work and think tank research, it seemed as if the universe might be inviting me back to climb back on board and once more take on some real work. I bit its hand off!

People were so helpful – clinicians, organisations, individuals, all equally frustrated with the state of treatment currently available in the UK. So many individuals contributed to helping me to pull together a small staff capable of handling such a challenge. I was able to advertise a job through one of the registering bodies in America and a very impressive woman, rich in experience in this area, responded almost immediately. She came over from America to visit the property, as did a lot of local therapists and, gradually, with the help of an experienced local supervisor, we were able to pull together a crack team to take on the task of attempting to replicate the treatment success of the trauma clinic in Arizona. The plan was simply to copy what they had done as faithfully as possible. I saw my job as being the messenger boy, delivering the treatment protocol as the inside man, and as the general factotum setting up the business side. When I had left the trauma clinic, a number of the staff there, from top to bottom urged me to tell people about these new treatments and encouraged me to get involved personally in making change happen in our industry. I drew great comfort and heart from their kind words. They were right that their pioneering treatment needed to become more widely available. I was in a great rush to play my part in that. In fact, so spurred on was I, I think I must have still been powered by that righteous indignation, that rage I still had about my suffering and my treatment, but at least it was a rage that was constructive. Still, being in a rush and treating trauma are not a great combination. This, alas, I was going to learn the hard way.

One way or another I was able to knock all of the details together during the spring and summer of 2011 and we were due to open the clinic that September. There were few outstanding details as we careened towards our beginning. Some of the support staff were not in place yet and there were on-going discussions about extending the lease on the house, but at the same time some major obstacles had been overcome. We had planning permission, the American therapist was coming over to live in Britain and work at the clinic full time. Our other therapists were less experienced in comparison but promising all the same, and excited, and we had a great supervisor, one of the original students of these methods. I was manically being the bloke who did everything else, with no financing or support for the business other than the woman who gave us the house and her generous family, but grateful for this wonderful opportunity. I own, I may have been spinning perhaps several plates too many but I was enjoying it.

It had been a long time since I had been able to deploy these skills which had become second nature to me during my entrepreneurial youth. I was having fun and feeling hopeful. Good things were happening with good people and we were setting ourselves up to help some others. I felt the wind of the universe in my sails and allowed myself to feel that this might actually be my calling; that this could be the turnaround which could make sense of all the pain I had been through; that we might transplant that healing experience to the UK and save some lives over here. It was an exciting time and yet nerve wracking. I was working sometimes all day, seven days a week, and I think this was a shock for my family. I'd gone from the being a poor substitute for a nanny to someone who was now never available. I don't think it was easy for them, nor that they entirely trusted this manic burst of activity. But whatever the private cost, I was working and this held out some promise for providing for my family. We all made the best of it and got on with it, fingers crossed for a good outcome for all parties.

Finally we were on the home straight. The last of the Ikea furniture had been assembled, the knives and forks were all in place, the cushions set out, the office and staff flat just perfect, all kindly arranged by my wife's well practiced home-making skills. It was going to be a lovely place in which to work and to heal. By the end of the week, everything was to our liking. We left ourselves a day, just in case, but we didn't need it. We were all set by Thursday afternoon. On Saturday our therapist was due to fly in from Boston. On Monday and Tuesday our first four patients were arriving. We had made it; we were there, and I couldn't wait to get started. Shattered, I returned home on Thursday afternoon, grateful for the day in hand, looking forward to a few moments of doing nothing for once. But I didn't get to rest for long.

At 6pm an email came through from the landlord's solicitors demanding that we immediately vacate the premises because it was not being used as a private house. This was true, but also a complete nonsense. Although I had not been party to the original lease, the house had been let to the woman who offered it to me for the exact purpose we were now using it for. I had met the landlord and talked all about our plans. He had cooperated fully with the planning consent which had been done through his recommended contact, and he had talked of his desire to see people being helped, since he himself had some experience of helping people in recovery. Now, at the eleventh hour and fifty-nine minutes, he wanted us out, immediately and inexplicably. Fortunately, there are laws about this kind of thing, so although I was shocked, frightened and disappointed, I knew that we could not be kicked out of a property for which we had a valid lease, not for a while at least. Not legally anyway. Just as I was reeling from this, I took a call from a member of the family who had originally leased the house. They were receiving threats of unending law suits from the landlord, and they had decided to cut their losses and to give the house back to him the following day!

It was about nine o'clock at night and I was apoplectic. They were to have been part owners of the business and had spent a large sum of money getting the house ready, not to mention renting it for months for nothing. Yet now, in the face of one unpleasant phone call from an angry man, they had simply thrown in the towel, without even consulting a lawyer. I could not believe it, but also I was worried that there might be nothing I could do about it. I was by now a director of the company which had rented the house, but if my partners simply left and handed over the keys, that would largely be that. I did know that possession is really everything in these kinds of property disputes. I hardly slept and early the next morning I set out for the house. I arrived there to find my worst fears realised.

The woman who had first contacted me was packing up her things to move out and the family were helping her. Worst still, an intimidating six-foot man was moving my possessions out of the house into the road in front. He had started with a huge American fridge which, scarily, he was proving able to manhandle on his own. I had taken legal advice on the way up and, although the landlord had never finally completed the amendments to the lease to allow this trade at the property, he had taken money for the rent on the knowledge that it was happening and therefore had no case to argue. Furthermore, if I did not agree to the surrender of the lease, it was not valid, since it required both directors of the company to do so. I planned to stay at the house all weekend and to open the clinic as planned on the Monday morning. There seemed little that the landlord could do, however determined he was. Still, as the morning progressed, the family who had leased the property and I were bombarded with threats, legal and otherwise and, caught in the middle of this, they just couldn't get out of there quickly enough.

As the situation became more fraught, I called the police and we ended up spending the morning inside the house in a Mexican standoff between three policemen, two security guards, the family, myself and a ping-pong of legal calls on the phone. Finally my lawyer said that the landlord's lawyer had accepted that his position was not legal and that he was going to advise him in the next five minutes to call off his man and to leave me in peace at the property. The relief was extraordinary. I had been walking round in a daze, looking at this perfectly readied property, remembering all the work that had gone into it, devastated at the work that would not be now happening at it. It was all so perfect and starting tomorrow, surely what had just occurred had all been a bad dream? How could all of this be taken away from me now, just as I was managing to get back on my feet? You could not have made it up. So when the next call came, I was unprepared because I had thought I was at last safe. I could not have been more wrong.

The landlord did call his man, but the instruction did not vary. He wanted me out and his man in. I informed the police, explaining to them my legal advice. Reasonably enough, they informed me that they were not lawyers and that from the paperwork we had, only the woman who had offered me the property was listed as a resident of the house and she was outside packing up all her belongings into her car. The police sergeant told me that he wanted me to leave the property and to pursue the matter through the courts. His only concern was that there should not be a "breach of the peace" and he advised me to leave for my own protection. He could not stand there all day and make sure nothing worse happened and since he was a policeman, and not a lawyer, there was only so much he could do with tempers so frayed. I was naively astonished. I suppose they considered that they would be doing me a favour getting me out of there just in case anything did indeed get worse, and perhaps they were right. This was also becoming no environment in which to start a trauma clinic. I left in shock, grabbed a couple of computers – which was all that I could salvage at the time – and drove out of the gates, watching my possessions being loaded into the drive behind me.

It was Friday afternoon. My one full-time therapist was on her way to catch her flight out of Boston to come and live and work at a house away from which I had just been escorted by the police, despite owning a legal lease to be there. I had four patients due, who were currently spending the weekend preparing to try to reclaim their lives in treatment starting from Monday. As I drove out of those gates, my world collapsed around me yet again. My apparently misplaced conceit at being asked by 'the universe' to pass on this work to the world crumbled into ash in a morning. The promises I had so sincerely given others as I spun the plates to set the place up, came back to haunt me.

I watched my dreams disappear into nothing in my rear-view mirror and went home to face the music, broken before they had even begun.

EPILOGUE

The clinic survived and is still helping people to recover from a variety of conditions, all of which we now see as being rooted in one condition, a dysregulated nervous system. I called it Khiron House, Khiron being the Greek myth of the wounded healer. It is an acknowledgement of my own damaged parts and a reminder to those of us who work there never to stand apart from our patients. We are all on a continuum and on the same journey. Some of us just left on earlier trains.

Now, a little over three years since it was established, I realise quite what a huge task it was to undertake and sometimes look back on its traumatic birth as a kind of test: was I serious about taking on such a challenge? Every time someone thanks me with tears in their eyes for setting up the clinic and wonders out loud what on earth would have happened to them if it didn't exist, I remember why I was so determined to make it work. This was exactly how I felt leaving the original trauma unit in Arizona.

When I hear my own story replicated in their most sincere and intimate words, I know that it was worth it. My life was handed back to me in the desert, and now it is on loan to others. That is just as it should be; and unavoidable.

The story of how we got from that terrible morning to where we are now with the clinic is the opening narrative of the next book in this series, Why We Do What We Do (Over And Over Again) and How To Change. In a nutshell, we had to rebuild it from the ground up again, with new staff and a new location, and all of that in a week before we lost our first clients. I can only look back on it and believe that we were very lucky, either that or it was just one of those things that was 'meant to be'.

Whilst the clinic survived, my marriage was not so fortunate. So many of our relationships when we have trauma are founded on the basis of an unseen bond between the survivors of terrible traumas and childhood relationships. Without our even knowing it, there can become a need to set in place compensations for our wounds. As both my wife and I healed, we renegotiated those bonds. It is not always clear where trauma ends and health begins. A healthy self in the end demands a healthy relationship and the difficulties which invariably arise as the nervous system recalibrates are sadly unavoidable. But at least everything now makes sense, for both of us. We are not fighting in the dark, but negotiating in the light. It is hard, painful and heart-breaking at times. But at least it is true, finally, and honest.

In the end I also spoke to my father about my concerns regarding his behaviour after my mother died. He was kind enough not to dismiss the idea that

I had been sexually abused during that tumultuous time. However, he was clear that he was not the perpetrator, which I have accepted. He pointed out that I had passed through many hands during that year and that I might be mistaken as to the identity of this 'father figure'. This is true and his reality deserves consideration and respect. This is not a witch hunt, just an explanation. I am fortunate enough to have got out of this what I needed from within my own nervous system. I don't need any more validation from anyone else externally. It is clear that a very deep part of me believed that he was the perpetrator and that this has run my behaviour in relation to him ever since. Whether or not that correlates to something done by him, or something done by someone else interpreted by me as 'the father', sadly, is of no concern to the body. My biology needed to complete something; why was irrelevant.

Whoever it was, I wouldn't judge him anymore. I now understand each and every person on this planet from a different perspective. It is the deep biological crisis of the nervous system which drives people's behaviour. I'm not perfect either and it helps me when I remember my own failings not to judge too harshly those who have also failed me. I am left with the priceless gift of being able to find compassion for my abuser. Wherever he is, whatever he is doing now, he will have these same problems that I did, and for that I have only heart and forgiveness. No-one wants to be sick and no-one wants to hurt others. We are all prisoners of our biology but now we live on the cusp of an era when we can stop punishing people for this and start to release them from their own private, anatomical jails, however horrific their acts might be.

Likewise family members, therapists, institutions, doctors and friends. They all did their best to help me and I don't judge them either. The hospitals which failed me routinely help countless others to sustained recoveries. The paradox of this just reveals one of the greatest problems in mental health, that of the right treatment being applied to the wrong patient. This new evolution of treatments will make that less likely, new treatments being more broadly and more routinely effective. The biggest problem remains that either the therapists or the patient are very often denied any actual choice about whether or not to treat or to accept treatment. Either politics or money gets in the way and so real choice, assessing which problem needs which solution, is often hard to find. (Get Stable is my initiative to end this dynamic in the state sector, with both therapist and client opting into the treatment before delivery).

For families, the breakdown of a loved one, through mental illness, addiction or behaviour can be a terrifying, lonely time. Because treatments are so often utterly unreliable, it seems to be so unsatisfactory and so difficult to try to navigate the various options available. Free help can be inappropriate and Kafkaesque in its confusion and lack of transparency. Private help is crucifyingly expensive, and not risk free. For family members it can become a total gamble trying to figure out when to stick and when to twist, relying on nothing but blind luck to try to forge a sane path through all the different professional opinions. My family were not spared. Bottom line is that without their agreement to pay for my treatment, I would very likely be dead by now. I will always be grateful for that, despite the dramas, which no doubt at times were almost as painful on their side as they were on mine.

Various other people either tried to help me, or did in fact help me greatly, with everything from well wishes, to some robust honesty, from offering actual cash to free treatment. What people could do for me they often did: strangers, professionals, even the lifelong friends whom I had abandoned but who in the end were concerned for me anyway. For all of it, I remain grateful. My need at certain points was almost infinite, which is unattractive, but nonetheless, people helped me anyway.

Written large on every piece of stationary, every wall, every bumper sticker at the hospital I was in in Arizona was the strapline, "Recovery becomes Reality". In my journey beyond that tortured first five weeks of treatment there, into the new paradigm of modern treatment at their trauma clinic, I can see that in the truth of restoring the nervous system, a new maxim emerges: "Reality becomes Recovery". It was in becoming able to listen to and to accept the truth contained in my body that I was able to settle my biology back into something like the place it was born to be.

And in this truth I face the world naked, stripped down, raw, unvarnished by denial. It is a horrible, daunting, ongoing task that confronts me: to rebuild myself and my life from such shattered yet priceless raw material. First came the rebooting of my biological self that had crashed so badly, then a slow return to actually taking care of myself. From these two steps, a more healthy way of relating to others became possible, and then finally I was able to investigate my true place in this world, to glimpse from a place of internal health and security who I was really 'meant' to be.

This book is about the sabotage I wrought in my own life, both consciously and unconsciously, and how through gaining help for the consequences of that sabotage, I found out in turn what all of my own baffling behaviour and ineffective treatment really meant. Through my pain was born an understanding and that understanding gave my experience meaning, in both senses of the word.

My reversal of fortune was the most clichéd journey of all. In losing everything – money, health, my mind, family, relationships and even the will to live – I was fortunate enough to turn the vicious cycle of trauma repetition on its head and to start again, hopefully initiating a virtuous cycle of self-care and other-care, built from the inside out, with truth, honesty and integrity, as opposed to from the outside in, like a gilded castle waiting to fall out of the sky.

And I know that one day, grudgingly, and with great resistance, but inevitably, I will say that most boring, bland, maddening, meaningless statement all serial survivors inevitably fall back upon once the storm has passed: that it was the best thing that ever happened to me; and that I'm truly grateful for my journey, the truth it has revealed to me, and the priceless opportunity it bestowed upon me to pass it on to others.

Do likewise.

RESOURCES

If you, a friend or a relation are having any of the problems I suffered in this book, you might want to know more about how to get better, the details of my treatment and what your options are for getting access to the same.

The next book in this series, Why We Do What We Do (Over And Over Again) and How To Change, outlines the theories behind the treatment and explains what happened in this story from that perspective. All of the baffling, crazy, destructive episodes of this tale actually make perfect sense once you understand the depth of my relationship with my anatomy, neurobiology and nervous system. It is designed to be a self-help version of the Khiron House treatment programme and a guide to implementing these methods for yourself at home. I hope that it will make this work accessible to as many people as need it.

If you need more help than that, whether you are looking for a local counsellor, or need immediate residential treatment, there are a number of options for you to consider.

The trauma unit I went to in Arizona closed down in May 2013. The larger hospital which owned it was itself bought by a private equity firm who installed new management. It was decided that the buildings could be used more profitably for adolescents.

The residential clinic which I founded in Oxford, UK, however continues this modality of work in a residential setting. It began as a faithful copy of the clinic in Arizona and, both in its feel and in its results, appears to have been successful in replicating the original clinic. We work every day to continue to innovate and to improve it.

We have found that in working with both trauma and attachment we have benefited from making Sensorimotor Psychotherapy our primary treatment modality at the clinic alongside the other methods mentioned above. This is now the tent pole of our mixed modality programme in the clinic.

We expanded from the residential programme to offer an out-patient service in London, again drawing on these methods of Sensorimotor Psychotherapy, Somatic Experiencing and EMDR. We deliver both group work and individual one-to-one sessions in this programme.

For people resonating with this story and looking for help from these methods, there are a number of ways to find this work without having to come to me or to Khiron House for help. The best resource is to Google the three methods mentioned above and add into your search your own location. Equally you can find your local association for these modalities online and usually that will list practitioners in private practice in your area. The cost and availability can vary considerably.

The hardest part of all of this is that almost all of this work is in the private sector and therefore needs paying for by the people who need the help, often those least able to help themselves. If you are in the UK you might be able to get an NHS referral to Khiron House, but it is rare. We offer a few concessionary rates for our groups in London and many independent practitioners also offer concessions for their private practice treatments.

My social enterprise, Get Stable, is an initiative to allow the greater variety of treatments available in the private sector (to people with money) to be available via NHS commissioning in a safe, value-for-money way. If you are lucky enough to live in an area which commissioned Get Stable, you might be able to get access to some of this work through our network of UK therapists listed on that website too.

Some people can only manage to get help from books or online resources, but even that can be a life changing resource. I am hoping that my next book in this series fills that gap, but also look for titles by Pat Odgen, Babette Rothschild, Francine Shapiro, Dan Siegel, Peter Levine, and Stephen Porges. Between them they know pretty much everything that is going to define the next century of radical change in what we think we understand to be 'mental health' care (it isn't – it's in the body!).

And if you need more help, just ask. Call me on +44 (0)20 7467 8368 or send me an email to help@khironhouse.com and I will do what I can to get you going in the right direction.

I am here to help.

ABOUT THE AUTHOR

Benjamin Fry, born to an American mother and English father, was brought up in London. He has been a male model, entrepreneur, television presenter, author and psychotherapist. He currently runs Khiron House, a mental health service which has an outpatient clinic in Harley Street and a residential clinic in Oxford, where he also lives. This is his third book.

Also by Benjamin Fry

Books:
What's Wrong With You
Spendsmart

Audio books:
How to Be Happy
How to Be Rich

Made in the USA
Las Vegas, NV
04 November 2022